# Roses

M000022322

*Frances Tenenbaum, Series Editor*

 HOUGHTON MIFFLIN COMPANY

*Boston • New York* 1999

# Roses

## Easy Plants for More Beautiful Gardens

Produced by Storey Communications, Inc.
Pownal, Vermont

Copyright © 1999 by Houghton Mifflin Company

All rights reserved

For information about permission to reproduce selections from
this book, write to Permissions, Houghton Mifflin Company,
215 Park Avenue South, New York, New York 10003.

*Taylor's Guide* is a registered trademark of Houghton Mifflin
Company.

Library of Congress Cataloging-in-Publication Data is
available.
ISBN 0-395-87334-7

Printed in the United States of America

WCT 10 9 8 7 6 5 4 3 2 1

# Contents

# INTRODUCTION

Roses represent love and beauty. Their colors and fragrance create the standard by which many other flowers are measured. Cultivated around the world for perfume, roses have a sweet and unforgettable scent. Roses come in most colors except blue. Yet many would-be rose gardeners believe they require constant care: pruning, deadheading, training, feeding, and lavish doses of sprays and chemicals. Roses do require attention, particularly the hybrid teas, but their glorious flowers make all your efforts worthwhile.

The roses in this book were chosen because they are tried-and-true, proven performers under the conditions stated with each selection. Their flowers are lovely, each with a distinctive character and some with fragrances that linger in your memory long after the last rose of autumn has faded away.

## The World of Roses

To simplify your understanding of this large and variable family of flowers, the featured roses have been divided into six groups.

*Species roses* grow naturally in the wild. Typically, they produce flowers with five petals and come true from seed. They tend to be vigorous, ranging plants, ideal for settings where you want them to spread out and fill with blooms.

*Shrub roses* is a class for roses that don't fit into the other groups. Some were bred by crossing sweet-scented, many-petaled, old garden roses and more recent hybrid teas or other modern roses. In this category are ground cover roses, hybrid rugosa roses, English roses, and others.

*Old garden roses* are those that were grown in the nineteenth century and earlier; they were mostly cultivated before 1867, when the first hybrid tea rose was developed. They are further subdivided into approximately thirteen classes including gallica, alba, Bourbon, tea, damask, and centifolia. Usually they bloom once each growing season in early summer, finishing before the onslaught of Japanese beetles that devour other roses in much of the country.

*Climbers* and *ramblers,* with training, can grow over trellises, arbors, and buildings. They can also stand alone to form a lush, free-form mound.

*Floribundas, grandifloras,* and *hybrid teas* are popular rose groups. While the bushy, cluster-flowering floribundas and grandifloras are a fairly recent development, hybrid teas date back to the mid-eighteenth century. Hybrid tea roses are prized for their elegant high-centered blooms, long stems, and wide choice of colors as well as their often delightful fragrance.

*Miniature roses* are very small. While a climbing miniature rose may reach 10 feet tall, the typical mini is 8 to 24 inches high. The flowers, leaves, and even thorns are all in scale with one another.

## How to Use This Book

Let the pictures that follow inspire you to grow roses of your own. Or if you already grow roses from one or two categories, study the entries for unfamiliar plants and try something new. Why garden, after all, if you can't have fun?

Whichever rose you choose, whether it climbs over an arbor or edges a little flower bed, savor it. Learn about roses firsthand by growing them, nurturing them, moving them when they do not thrive, replacing them if they die, all the time increasing your knowledge of and joy in what many consider the most perfect of flowers. Included in the box that accompanies each rose photo is information about the necessary growing conditions and vital statistics of each rose. The box also includes bloom time, using the designations common to reference books, rose nursery catalogs, and plant tags. Naturally, the exact date or month varies depending on where you garden and that year's weather conditions.

*Early:* This means the rose blooms in late spring or early summer.

*Midseason:* The rose begins blooming in early to midsummer.

*All Season:* It blooms continuously, from early summer through fall.

# Caring for Your Roses

Individual growing requirements and suggestion for care are included with each rose, but there are some general cultural and maintenance procedures that apply to all roses.

*Siting:* Take into account the shade tolerance, height, and width of the roses you choose to grow. Leave room for the shrubs to mature.

*Preparing the Hole:* Dig an ample hole, 2 feet wide and deep (somewhat less for smaller plants), and amend the soil with compost, well-rotted manure, leaf mold, dampened peat moss, or store-bought humus. If you're inclined to measure, use at least one part organic material to two parts soil. If your soil is heavy with clay, use sand mixed with humus or crumbly rotted manure to increase the drainage. Add a couple of handfuls of bonemeal or superphosphate to the hole to promote root growth. To avoid compacted soil, don't plant your rose when the soil is wet.

*Planting:* For a bareroot rose, soak the roots of the plant in water at least overnight or for 24 hours. Then set it in the hole on a crown of mounded soil and spread out the roots evenly. For a containerized rose, pop it out of its pot and tease apart the roots, especially if they're congested. Put it in a hole that is larger than the pot it came in. In either case, cover the plant so the bud graft is buried under 1 inch of soil in northern areas; it should be about 1 inch above the soil surface in warm regions. With your hands, pack the soil around the base of the plant. Water deeply.

*Mulching:* After planting, spread a 2-inch layer of mulch such as rotted manure or compost over the root zone to retain moisture and keep the soil cool. Renew in fall after the ground has frozen and again each spring when leaves begin to emerge.

*Fertilizing:* Once established, mound composted manure around each shrub. You may also fertilize lightly with a complete rose food in spring as buds begin to break and again after the first bloom begins to fade.

*Pruning:* Before bud break, remove dead, damaged, or crowded canes. Information about how much to prune the healthy canes of individual roses is noted with each entry; the best time is generally while the bush is dormant, in late winter or early spring. To shape a rosebush, just trim the branch tips by making an angled cut ¼ inch above an outward-facing bud.

*Pest Control:* If you live in an area of lush lawns, then Japanese beetles may be a problem. Pick them off by hand in the cool of the morning when they won't fly away, dropping them into a cup of soapy water to drown them. Spray grassy areas with milky spore or predatory nematodes. Rose stem girdler is a small green beetle that lays its eggs near the base of rose canes. When the soft-bodied grubs hatch, they feed on the stems, causing a swollen area, sometimes accompanied by splitting of the bark. To control, promptly prune out and destroy infested canes.

*Disease Control:* Roses get mildew and black spot, among other maladies. Always remove and dispose of affected leaves and canes; in fall, rake and remove dead leaves from around the shrub. Spray susceptible bushes each spring just as leaves are emerging and again throughout the season as needed. See individual entries for specific information.

*Cold Weather:* Determine the cold hardiness of the roses you like to see if they coincide with the area where you live. Most likely, your property has microclimates where tender plants can remain protected and relatively warm year-round, while others are fully exposed to the elements. In Zones 6 and north, protect roses from winter damage by mounding 12 inches of soil or mulch over the base of each plant in fall after the ground has frozen. The addition of rose cones, or straw and chicken wire, may also be warranted, and helps protect the plants from the devastating effects of freeze and thaw cycles. The following spring, do not bare the roses until danger of frost is past.

# PASTURE ROSE
## Species (*Rosa carolina*)

Zones: 4–8

Size: 3–6 ft. tall, 3–6 ft. wide

Bloom Time: Mid-season

Bloom Width: 2 in.

Fragrance: Moderate

Thorniness: Slight

The pasture rose is a species native to the eastern United States. In midseason, the small flowers appear singly, for the most part, although some grow in small clusters. The rose has sweetly scented blossoms with five medium pink petals that are followed by small, bright red hips in fall. Pasture rose has a strong suckering habit, and it forms a thicket if its growth is left unchecked. Its canes are fairly smooth, though not thorn-free. This vigorous plant is disease-free and winter hardy except in extremely cold areas.

### HOW TO GROW
Sited in full sun, pasture rose has deep green leaves and abundant flowers. In dappled shade, the growth is more open with fewer blossoms. It is an adaptable plant, thriving in the rich, loamy soils of upland forests and

prairies but growing equally well in sandy soils and coastal conditions. Amend clay soils with organic matter to improve drainage and inhibit compacting. Once established, the plant produces many suckers. Remove up to half of these each spring to maintain a neat, mounded habit and increase flower production.

### HOW TO USE

Because of its naturally wild appearance and tendency to grow densely, pasture rose works well at the edges of thickets or on property boundaries. In such settings, it can form a coarse, informal hedge away from the organized architecture of the home.

## Top Choices

- 'Plena' is a double rose with outer petals that whiten as they age; the plant is not quite as tall as the species.

- *R. laevigata,* Cherokee rose, is a Chinese species that has naturalized throughout the Southeast. Its large, white, single flowers are fragrant and are followed by showy hips.

- *R. palustris,* swamp rose, is another U.S. native that tolerates wetter soil than most roses. Its sweet-scented pink flowers appear late in the season.

- *R. villosa,* apple rose, has fragrant, pink, single flowers followed by showy hips that resemble small apples.

## FOR THE BIRDS

A rose with dense growth is a good choice for attracting birds because it provides a comfortable, protected nest site. You may observe robins, bluebirds, or quail. Don't be surprised to see sparrows, towhees, and cardinals nesting in the tightly woven branches of larger rosebushes.

Rose hips are an important food source for some birds during barren winter months. A disease-resistant rose such as the pasture rose is best because you won't need to use chemical sprays that harm birds.

When selecting your rose, look for a plant that will produce small hips such as the pasture rose. Large, showy ones are too big for birds to eat.

## WHO CAN I TALK TO?

An excellent source of rose information is the American Rose Society; P.O. Box 30,000; Shreveport, LA 71130-0030 or telephone 318-938-5402. If you have a question of a local nature, such as which roses are easiest to grow in your area, the organization has a national network of consulting rosarians and can refer you to one nearby.

# SWEETBRIAR ROSE
## Species (*Rosa eglanteria*)

Zones: 5–9

Size: 8–10 ft. tall, 8 ft. wide

Bloom Time: Early, with no repeat

Bloom Width: 1–1½ in.

Fragrance: Moderate

Thorniness: Very

Sweetbriar rose is a familiar sight in the hedgerows of its native England. Known by several names— eglantine, sweetbriar, and Shakespeare's rose—it bears clusters of petite flowers with five pink petals and flashy yellow stamens. These occur early in the season with no repeat, and have a sweet rose scent; they are followed later in the season by clusters of large (about an inch in diameter), scarlet, oval hips. A special feature of this rose is its foliage, which smells of green apples, especially when brushed against or crushed. Warm, moist winds and rain also release the fragrance of the leaves. The extremely thorny canes are long, upright, arching, and covered with small, glossy green leaves. This vigorous plant is disease-free.

## HOW TO GROW

Site sweetbriar rose in full sun, in well-drained soil amended with large amounts of organic matter. It needs neutral to slightly alkaline conditions. Spring pruning creates a compact, impenetrable hedge, but it sacrifices the best flowering shoots. You may remove some older shoots in July after blooming to give newer shoots the space to mature and grow (note that young foliage has a stronger scent).

## HOW TO USE

Sweetbriar rose makes a terrific barrier and privacy hedge because of its dense, upright, arching growth and thorny canes. A classic cottage-garden plant, this rose looks best rambling with other shrubs and flowers at the garden's edge, where it can serve as a transition to the wilder part of your property.

## *Top Choices*

- 'Hebe's Lip' is a fragrant hybrid sweetbriar with semidouble white blossoms and gold stamens. It stands 4 feet tall and blooms early and abundantly, with no repeat.

- 'Lord Penzance' has soft, yellow, single blooms, borne on an extremely vigorous bush that quickly reaches 8 feet high and wide.

## MAKING A PROPER
## PRUNING CUT

While cutting into a healthy rose branch may cause a moment of trepidation, the positive results will make any anxiety worthwhile.

**1** Buy quality pruning shears, and keep them sharp. Inexpensive and dull ones crush or mash rather than slice.

**2** Make your cut just above a healthy, outward-facing bud or a promising side branch. The goal is to inspire new growth that grows away from the center of the bush, not into it.

Conventional wisdom counsels about ¼ inch above, but do your best. If you cut too far from a bud, the result is a dead stub that may invite disease into the stem. If you cut too close to a bud, it can dry out or be damaged by freezing weather.

**3** Always cut at a slant to the stem, at about a 45-degree angle. Such cuts dry out faster after a rain, and too much dampness encourages disease.

**4** Ideally, the cut should slope downward toward the center of the bush.

# RED-LEAVED ROSE
## Species (*Rosa rubrifolia*)

Zones: 3–8

Size: 4–8 ft. tall, 4–6 ft. wide

Bloom Time: Early, with no repeat

Bloom Width: 1 in. or smaller

Fragrance: None

Thorniness: Slight

Why grow red-leaved rose, with its modest pink flowers? The answer lies in its foliage, a magnificent gray-green flushed with mauve and accented with maroon veins and stems. Moreover, the sunnier the location of your shrub, the more the leaves are suffused with an appealing, rich copper tint. Red-leaved rose is, in fact, a rose with year-round interest. In winter, you will admire the beautiful red to reddish brown canes, which are also practically thorn-free. In early summer, tiny, delicate, five-petaled pink flowers with white eyes and prominent yellow stamens appear. By autumn, the handsome bush bears big bunches of scarlet, 1-inch hips. Throughout spring, summer, and fall, the striking foliage is always an eye-catching addition to the garden. This rose stands up to 8 feet tall with an open, upright, arching habit. It is winter hardy and disease-free.

## HOW TO GROW

In northern areas, plant red-leaved rose in full sun; plant in part shade in warmer regions. It will thrive when given a spot in well-worked garden soil that has been amended with rotted manure or other organic matter. Red-leaved rose is easy to care for once established. It requires no pruning other than removal of dead or damaged canes. Although this species is largely pest- and disease-free, during hot, dry summers the foliage can turn color prematurely and drop; spider mites can also be a problem under these conditions.

## HOW TO USE

Red-leaved rose prefers a cool site with good air circulation. North or northeast exposures on gently sloping land are best, so long as there is enough sun. Because of its handsome foliage, keep red-leaved rose near your cutting garden so you remember to use it to enhance bouquets. Or place it in a mixed border, underplanted with perennials in reds and purples to harmonize with the warm color statement made by its red-tinged leaves.

## *Top Choice*

- *R.* 'Carmenetta' is a 1930 cross between red-leaved rose and *R. rugosa*, which, alas, gave this hybrid thorns and a rougher aspect; it also gave the plant a tougher constitution. It may do better by the seashore in light, sandy soil and is also more heat tolerant than red-leaved rose. Otherwise, 'Carmenetta' has leaves and hips similar to those of the red-leaved rose.

## PRUNING DEAD CANES

Species roses are all very hardy. They never require the extensive pruning and attention that are often demanded by some other roses, but the occasional removal of dead canes helps encourage good health and fresh new growth. If the plant is thorny, protect yourself. Note that you can do this chore at any time, but early spring, before the plant fills with foliage and blooms, is easiest.

**1** Acquire long-handled loppers that are sharp enough to cut through deadwood with little resistance.

**2** Identify dead branches to be removed by tracing them down to the base of the plant or by examining the plant's base.

**3** Always cut off a dead cane as cleanly as possible at its base.

**4** Carefully extract the dead canes from the bush and discard.

# BEACH ROSE
## Species (*Rosa rugosa*)

Zones: 2–9

Size: 3–6 ft. tall, 6 ft. wide

Bloom Time: All season

Bloom Width: 2–3 in.

Fragrance: Strong

Thorniness: Very

*R*osa rugosa is a familiar sight along the New England coast. Some call it the beach rose because it thrives in harsh seaside conditions. Others say it's the Japanese rose because it originated in Japan (and in Korea and northern China). Most gardeners who grow this rose agree that, whatever its name, this rugged plant adds both heady fragrance and beauty to the garden. Perfumed blossoms of magenta pink with five to twelve petals open from long, pointed buds. These repeat from spring until frost. Canes are thick, upright, and robust—and bristling with thorns. The dark green leaves are leathery and wrinkled with deep-set veins; they turn yellow in fall. The fat, round hips measure about an inch in diameter This rose is disease-free and winter hardy to -50°F and stands up to 6 feet tall with a dense and spreading habit.

## HOW TO GROW

*Rosa rugosa* does best in full sun but also grows well in sites with some light afternoon shade. It thrives in adverse conditions, making it a good choice for areas with sandy soils, coastal gardens, or hot, dry sites. Plant in any well-drained soil. Fertilize by topdressing with rotted manure in spring and again in fall. Shear a hedge or windbreak each spring. This rose is occasionally troubled by rose stem girdler (prune out and destroy infested canes) and Japanese beetles (handpick).

## HOW TO USE

Because of its dense habit and its thick, prickly stems, *Rosa rugosa* makes an impenetrable hedge. It can also bring summerlong contrast and color to the typical foundation planting of conifers and broadleaved evergreens. Rugosas are suitable for mixed beds and borders. They thrive in difficult conditions, such as near a busy road in poor soil with exposure to pollution, or in the path of harsh, salty winds at the seaside.

## Top Choices

- *R. rugosa rubra* and *R. rugosa alba* are, respectively, deep magenta and white forms. Both are strongly scented and continuously in bloom. *Alba*'s potent scent recalls the fragrance of cloves. Both sport large hips in fall.

- *R.* 'Therese Bugnet' is an extremely hardy (to -40°F) hybrid rugosa and has clustered, double, medium pink, fragrant flowers.

## Taylor's Tips

### ROSE HIP JAM

Rose hips have a vitamin C content that is four hundred times greater than that of oranges. So they are a popular and practical ingredient in jams and jellies; the sweet-tart taste and aroma and pretty rose color are pluses.

To make rose hip jam:

> 4 cups rose-hip puree
> 5 cups sugar
> 1 tablespoon lemon juice

**1** Collect hips when they are firm and ripe or almost ripe, and gently wash them in clear, cool water.

**2** Prepare a puree by adding just enough water to cover the hips. Simmer until the hips are soft. Put the pulp through a food mill.

**3** Combine the pulp, sugar, and lemon juice. Bring the mixture to a boil, then reduce heat. Simmer until thickened and desired consistency is reached.

**4** Ladle jam into hot sterilized jars and seal.

*Makes two to three pints*

# Scotch Rose
## Species (*Rosa spinosissima*)

Zones: 4–9

Size: 1–4 ft. tall, spreading

Bloom Time: Early, with no repeat

Bloom Width: 2 in.

Fragrance: Slight

Thorniness: Very

Scotch rose is a tough, hardy rose with handsome flowers and a low, mounding, suckering habit. A profuse late-spring bloomer, this shrub bears small, lightly but sweetly scented blossoms that are usually creamy white, sometimes blushed pink or yellow. They appear early in the season and do not recur. The purple to black hips that follow are about 1 inch in diameter; some gardeners enjoy using them for holiday decorations. Scotch rose can tolerate dry, windy sites and grows well in sandy seaside conditions, where it behaves like a low ground cover, spreading freely by suckers. In garden soil, where it grows taller, it may become a 6-foot thicket of very thorny stems. The dull green leaves of this winter-hardy, disease-resistant rose are small and fernlike. (It is sometimes listed as *R. pimpinellifolia*.)

## HOW TO GROW

Plant this shrub in full sun to light shade in any well-drained soil. It will do well on a gravelly slope as well as in the relative luxury of the garden. Maintenance is minimal. Once a year, prune out dead or damaged canes. During hot, dry summers the small leaves sometimes get a mild case of powdery mildew. In these same conditions spider mites are also occasionally seen. Neither of these problems seems to bother the plant.

## HOW TO USE

Because of its ability to grow in poor soil and adverse conditions, Scotch rose is an excellent choice for a seaside garden or a windswept bank, where its suckering habit can serve as a low ground cover and barrier to people and animals alike. It also works well where low maintenance is a necessity.

## Top Choices

- *R. spinosissima* was used by Kordes, the German rose breeder, as a parent for 'Frühlingsgold', a shrub rose he introduced in 1937. This hardy, vigorous shrub bears 3-inch-wide, light yellow flowers and grows up to 10 feet tall and 4 feet wide with an arching habit. It is a good plant for the back of the border.

- *R.* 'Frühlingsmorgen' is very similar to 'Frühlingsgold', but its petals are pink at the edges and palest yellow toward the center.

## TRANSPLANTING A ROSE

If a rose doesn't look quite as attractive as you thought it would in a particular spot, or if it outgrows its location, transplanting is in order. This does not have to be a traumatic experience for the plant. Just make sure you undertake the operation at the best time—while the rose is still dormant in early spring or late winter.

**1** Water the soil deeply the day before transplanting.

**2** Prepare an ample hole in the new location (18 inches wide and deep, or more), with soil and amendments to one side so you'll be ready to backfill.

**3** With a shovel or spade, dig a hole around the plant at least 18 inches in diameter—wider if it is particularly large.

**4** Gently remove the plant with its soil ball intact. Take care not to disturb the roots.

**5** Place the rose in its new location. Always replant at the same depth as it grew previously (there will be a soil line visible low down on the main stem or stems).

**6** Cut the top growth back by one-third to one-half. This reduces stress on the root system so it can devote itself instead to establishing the plant in the new spot.

# 'ABRAHAM DARBY'
## Shrub (English)

Zones: 6–9

Size: 4–6 ft. tall, 3–4 ft. wide

Bloom Time: Summer to frost

Bloom Width: 5 in.

Fragrance: Moderate

Thorniness: Very

Its large, spectacular blooms make 'Abraham Darby' a must for any rose garden. The color is a soft, luscious apricot tinged with yellow on the inside petals and pink on the outer petals. The heady fragrance is soft and fruity. This rose was introduced by English nurseryman David Austin in 1985 and named for a leader of Britain's industrial revolution. 'Abraham Darby' blooms repeatedly until frost brings the show to a halt. The blossoms last a long time in a vase or bowl as elegant, perfumed centerpieces. Just beware of the thorns, which may grow to 1 inch long.

### HOW TO GROW

As with most English roses, a sunny location in good soil is best. Prune plants in winter in mild areas and early spring in northern zones. Cut the canes back by one-quarter for a more attractively shaped plant but fewer, smaller flowers. 'Abraham Darby' is mildew resistant and mostly pest- and disease-free. It may show symptoms of rust in the East, Pacific Northwest, and mountain areas. To control, use a sulfur-based fungicide as needed. Always rake and remove dead leaves in fall.

## HOW TO USE

'Abraham Darby' is versatile in the land-scape. Planted alone, it makes an attractive specimen planting. Planted in groups of three, it makes a dramatic garden statement since the individual plants will eventually merge into one large mass of leaves and flowers. To create this effect, stake out an equilateral triangle with 2-foot sides and plant one rose at each corner. This rose also works well in a mixed border or as part of a rose bed featuring different rose varieties.

If you lack the space for a shrub rose in your garden, plant this rose as a low climber. The arching stems of 'Abraham Darby' can grow up to 10 feet tall when trained against a wall or trellis.

## Top Choices

- 'Charles Austin', an 'Aloha' descendant ('Abraham Darby' has the same parent), has cupped apricot flowers and a fruity fragrance.

- 'Golden Celebration', a relatively new Austin introduction, features heavy, cupped blooms that are deep golden and intensely fragrant.

## CARING FOR A NEW ROSE

No matter when you plant or trans-plant a rose, it will need special attention until it has fully recovered from the shock of the move.

- Water well on planting day and regularly thereafter, about once a week if there is no rain. A good soaking is always better than several light waterings.

- Lay down an inch or two of organic mulch at the plant's base; compost is ideal.

- Fertilize. Add a slow-release plant food to the hole, midway through the planting process. Or sprinkle a balanced fertilizer around the bush about once a month throughout summer, always watering it in well.

- Late-spring plantings can dry out due to warm and windy weather. Build an 8- to 10-inch mound of soil around the base of the plant. On a cloudy day (to minimize trauma), after new growth on the stems above is at least an inch long, gently wash away the mound with a stream of water.

- Use snow fencing or a similar barrier to shield new transplants from hot sun and drying winds.

- Plant in fall only in especially mild climates. Mound soil (see above) and wash away the fol-lowing spring.

# 'BLANC DOUBLE DE COUBERT'
## Shrub (Hybrid Rugosa)

Zones: 3–8

Size: 5–6 ft. tall, 4 ft. wide

Bloom Time: Early to midsummer, with later repeat

Bloom Width: 3 in.

Fragrance: Strong

Thorniness: Very

The old-fashioned charm of 'Blanc Double de Coubert', a French hybrid from 1892, comes from its snow white, intensely fragrant flowers. Scrolled buds are tinged with pink, and each semidouble blossom has eighteen to twenty-four petals and a strong, spicy scent. The first flush of flowers comes in early to midseason and is followed by a less floriferous repeat bloom. The leaves are a healthy, dark, leathery green and appear plentifully on thorny canes. 'Blanc Double de Coubert' has more than summer interest. In autumn, its foliage, which grows densely on the plant, turns bright yellow, and a few bright red hips emerge to replace the flowers. 'Blanc Double de Coubert' is extremely winter hardy and disease-free.

## HOW TO GROW

Although this rose prefers full sun, it can take some shade. Like all rugosas, it likes excellent drainage. Add a handful of bone-meal or superphosphate to the planting hole to promote root growth. To avoid compacted soil, don't plant your rose when the soil is wet. Once established, feed 'Blanc Double de Coubert' by mounding well-rotted manure around each shrub. This hybrid needs little to no pruning, but if you choose, trim to keep it in bounds. If you live in an area of lush lawns, Japanese beetles may be a problem. Pick them off by hand. Rose stem girdler may damage the canes; to control, prune out and destroy infested canes.

## HOW TO USE

'Blanc Double de Coubert' has a thick, spreading habit that lends itself to hedges; plant bushes 3 to 3½ feet apart. Thanks to its thorny canes, this rose can also function as an access barrier. It makes a tough, attractive foundation planting at a beach house battered with ocean spray. Similarly, this rose can be strategically sited near a home to obscure the view of a salted New England roadside. Because of its suckering habit, you can also use this rose to secure a precipitous bank or to form a large decorative bed.

## Top Choice

- 'Souvenir de Philemon Cochet' is a sport mutation of 'Blanc Double de Coubert', discovered in 1899. Its fully double white flowers are large, fragrant, and sometimes flushed pink at the center.

## NUTRIENTS: THE BIG THREE

For a long, healthy life, roses must have nitrogen, phosphorus, and potassium. These elements occur naturally in the soil. If there is a deficiency, it's up to you to provide supplements. Your roses will richly reward your care with lusher, healthier growth and more blooms.

Nitrogen (N) is the most important element. Without the right amount, roses have a poor start in spring, stunted growth, weak stems, few flowers, and yellow leaves. Too much causes more leaves than flowers and soft growth that is more susceptible to disease and vulnerable to frost damage. Add nitrogen to the soil using compost or fish emulsion.

Phosphorus (P) encourages a healthy root system as well as more and larger flowers. Your rose is not getting enough if its leaves turn dark green on top and purple below. Many fertilizers contain high amounts of this element, or you can add it solo in the form of bone-meal or superphosphate.

Potassium (K) deficiency results in poor flower production or color, weak stems, and wilting or yellow tips. As with phosphorus, potassium can be added to the soil in fertilizer or with 1 tablespoon per plant of potassium nitrate in early summer.

# 'BONICA'
## Shrub

**Zones:** 4–9

**Size:** 3–5 ft. tall, 5 ft. wide

**Bloom Time:** Mid-season, with excellent repeat

**Bloom Width:** 2 in.

**Fragrance:** None

**Thorniness:** Moderate

This rose offers a big payoff for little work. 'Bonica' is a healthy plant that blooms all summer long and is winter hardy to chilly Zone 4 (with protection). The flower's inner petals are medium pink, while the outer ones are a light silvery pink. Each double bloom has forty or more petals but barely any scent. The abundant flower clusters make a striking contrast with the small, dark green leaves against which they are set. These are followed in autumn by orange-red hips that, in many areas, persist well into winter. Introduced in France in 1982, 'Bonica' became the first shrub rose to be named an All-America Rose Selection (in 1987) and won a German award for exceptional hardiness and disease resistance.

## HOW TO GROW

Plant in full sun in well-drained soil amended with compost, manure, or leaf mold. Then add a layer of mulch 1 or 2 inches thick around the root zone. Prune in late winter or early spring while plants are still dormant. Prune hedges lightly, shaping the plants and removing damaged or old canes. 'Bonica' contracts black spot if preventative sprays are not applied. Spray with a solution of baking soda and water for light infections. If the disease has gained a foothold, spray with a solution of fungicidal soap and repeat in two weeks.

## HOW TO USE

'Bonica' makes an excellent tall ground cover or landscape rose. Gardeners especially prize its ability to choke out weeds. Grown as a dense hedge or massed in beds, 'Bonica' has an extended season of interest; after the blooming period has passed the plant sets attractive orange-red hips that last into winter. 'Bonica' also makes a handsome addition to the mixed border or stands on its own as a garden specimen. It works well in small gardens, where every plant counts, because of its rather modest size and because its growth is easily kept in check. Its medium pink flowers harmonize well with silver-leafed artemisias and blue campanulas, delphiniums, or salvias.

## Top Choice

- 'Royal Bonica' is an improved, somewhat taller version of 'Bonica'. It bears 2-inch, deep pink blooms in clusters of up to twenty flowers each.

## ROSE HIPS FOR CRAFTS

If you wish to collect rose hips for use in flower arrangements, wreaths, or swags, your goal is good color. Hips inevitably fade somewhat (some more than others), but drying them away from sunlight will help preserve their hue.

**1** In a dry, warm, airy, dim room, lay collected rose hips on newspaper so they aren't touching.

**2** Examine them daily to make sure they are drying properly and that the space is without excessive humidity. The process may take several weeks.

**3** Spray the dried hips with a fixing preservative (available from hobby stores). It should help them hold their color and prevent further moisture loss—and hence prevent shriveling.

# 'CAREFREE BEAUTY'
## Shrub

Zones: 4–9

Size: 5–6 ft. tall, 4 ft. wide

Bloom Time: Summer through fall

Bloom Width: 4 in.

Fragrance: Moderate

Thorniness: Moderate

'Carefree Beauty' is just that—a blithe belle that offers excellent all-season bloom, winter hardiness to Zone 4, and superb disease resistance. Its loosely formed blossoms are rosy pink, ovoid in shape, and appear in long-stemmed clusters that make for easy cutting. Each one is semidouble, with eighteen to twenty-four petals and a pleasant, fruity fragrance. Plentiful flower clusters appear on the upright, spreading shrub among smooth, apple green leaves. This is the best known of the tough hybrids developed by the late Dr. Griffith Buck.

### HOW TO GROW
Plant 'Carefree Beauty' in full sun. Unless the site already has good, rich soil, be sure to amend the planting hole with compost, rotted manure, or other organic

matter and a handful of bonemeal or super-phosphate fertilizer. If any canes sustain winter damage, they can be cut back nearly to the ground in spring just before the plant emerges from dormancy. Cut back remaining stems by one-quarter to one-third. 'Carefree Beauty' is generally disease resistant but may lose some leaves to black spot in summer. To control, apply a fungicidal soap or sulfur in spring as leaves are expanding and again a month later. If needed, apply again in summer.

## HOW TO USE

Its abundant blooms and tall, spreading growth make 'Carefree Beauty' appropriate for hedges and screens. Plant bushes 3 to 3½ feet apart. Or mass this rose in an uneven-numbered group for a handsome flowering accent in an all-shrub border. It can also stand on its own as a garden specimen. The decorative effect of 'Carefree Beauty' continues into winter with the presence of shiny orange-red hips. This low-maintenance plant works especially well in cold climates, where it usually survives without winter protection.

## Top Choice

- 'Country Dancer' is another terrific introduction from Dr. Buck (the late horticulture professor from Iowa State University at Ames). It sports large, fragrant, rose-red, double flowers that bloom all season. The shrub has vigorous canes and dark green leaves.

## SHAPING
# SHRUB ROSES

One of the attractive qualities of established shrub roses is that they require little care. However, selective pruning on occasion will result in a symmetrical plant with strong canes.

**1** At any time during the growing season, use sharp, long-handled loppers to neatly remove unwanted twigs and stubs. This will allow the bush to concentrate more energy on its remaining growth.

**2** In early spring, before the plants begin to bloom, prune back remaining growth. Reduce each cane to about two-thirds of its original length.

# 'CAREFREE WONDER'

## Shrub

Zones: 4–9

Size: 4 ft. tall,
3 ft. wide

Bloom Time: Mid-
season, with excellent
repeat

Bloom Width: 4–5 in.

Fragrance: Slight

Thorniness: Moderate

With medium pink petals, a creamy white reverse, and a white eye, each blossom of 'Carefree Wonder' looks like a hand-painted work of art. Its double, cupped blossoms have twenty-six petals that appear singly and in small clusters; its scent is light and sweet. Winter-hardy 'Carefree Wonder' is disease resistant and blooms continuously from midseason until frost. The neat but vigorous, bushy shrub has dense, medium green, semiglossy foliage and reddish thorns. Bred by Meilland of France, 'Carefree Wonder' captured the prestigious All-America Rose Selection Award in 1990.

### HOW TO GROW

'Carefree Wonder' prefers a site in full sun, and the more organic matter you can add to the planting hole, the better. It needs little or no pruning. Shape the plant a bit, if necessary, each spring before its buds begin to open. Japanese beetles are sometimes a problem; pick them off by hand and drop into a jar of soapy water. If you buy a commercial trap for Japanese beetles, set it up well away from your rosebushes so you don't inadvertently lure the beetles to your roses.

### HOW TO USE

Because 'Carefree Wonder' has a neat habit, it suits gardens of any size, an advantage for rose lovers with limited space. The shrub's trim growth and appearance make it appropriate not only for low-blooming hedges but also for foundation plantings. Massed in an uneven-numbered group, the floriferous 'Carefree Wonder' provides a dramatic color accent in the shrub border. It also makes a nice stand-alone garden specimen.

## Top Choice

- 'Carefree Delight', another rose bred by Meilland of France, won the All-America Rose Selection Award in 1996. Also a profuse bloomer, this shrub has darker, carmine pink, single flowers, also with white eyes. It grows wider than tall and has small, dense, dark green foliage and arching canes. It is extremely disease resistant and hardy.

## CHANGING YOUR SOIL'S pH

If you are planting a rose in your yard for the first time, make sure your soil is pH balanced. Use a soil test kit that measures pH. You can help balance your soil by regularly spreading compost or other organic matter. However, a quick change in the balance is also possible:

- If you find that your soil has a low pH, adding limestone will raise it and reduce acidity. It takes 5 pounds of dolomitic limestone spread over 100 square feet to raise the pH one point (more for clay soils, less for sand).

- To lower pH, work agricultural sulfur into the soil with a pitchfork or hoe, spreading as evenly as possible.

Once your soil is in balance, feed it a regular diet of compost to keep the pH at a healthy level.

## A CAREFREE SELECTION

Buying a plant of 'Carefree Wonder' grown on its own roots makes it even more winter hardy. Ask at the nursery. If you buy by mail, read the catalog copy carefully or give the nursery a call if you aren't sure what they're offering.

# 'CECILE BRUNNER'
## Shrub (Polyantha)

**Zones:** 5–9

**Size:** 3 ft. tall,
3 ft. wide

**Bloom Time:** Late
season, with excellent
repeat

**Bloom Width:** 1½ in.

**Fragrance:** Slight

**Thorniness:** Slight

Introduced in France in 1881, 'Cecile Brunner' is the classic, old-fashioned sweetheart rose. It bears perfectly formed flowers that begin as tiny, pointed, light pink buds. When open, the small, double blooms are lightly fragrant and look like miniature hybrid tea roses. They are borne first singly and later in sprays. 'Cecile Brunner' forms a bushy, rounded, spreading shrub with small, dark green, semiglossy foliage that is dense and plentiful, plus it is nearly thorn-free. Because of the flowers' petite size, sweet smell, and smooth stems, 'Cecile Brunner' is the consummate buttonhole rose.

### HOW TO GROW
'Cecile Brunner' prefers a site in full sun in northern areas and a sunny place with some light afternoon shade in regions where summers are hot. (Provide winter

protection in Zone 5 and colder parts of Zone 6.) Plant in soil amended with organic matter to increase fertility and improve drainage. For best flower production, prune back canes by one-half to two-thirds when leaves begin to emerge in spring. To stimulate flowering, fertilize with a balanced rose fertilizer after the first flush of flowers and prune lightly to remove spent flowers. This rose may suffer from some black spot in summer. Apply a fungicidal soap or sulfur as the leaves emerge, thereafter as needed. Its small leaves are subject to mite damage in late summer, especially when the weather is hot and dry. To control, spray plants with insecticidal soap, repeating every seven to ten days for a month.

### HOW TO USE

'Cecile Brunner' is a dwarf polyantha rose. Because of its small stature and tidy habit, it suits small gardens as well as large ones. The shrub's trim growth and appearance make it appropriate as a low-blooming hedge, as an edging, or massed in a small bed. You can also grow 'Cecile Brunner' in a pot, as long as you keep it well watered and fed.

## Top Choices

- 'Cecile Brunner, Climbing' makes an enchanting climber for a small space even though it has little repeat bloom. Its scrolled buds and hybrid tea blooms may be slightly larger than the bush variety, while its vigorous canes can grow as long as 25 feet. Zones 6 to 9.

- 'Cecile Brunner White' is a white sport.

## STARTING ROSES FROM CUTTINGS

Cuttings are a great way to add to your rose garden. Collect fresh new growth early in summer. Be sure you can commit to the constant vigilance cuttings will require in their early weeks and months.

**1** Use sharp pruners to cut young, green stem segments 4 to 6 inches long. Cut right below a leaf node, at a 45-degree angle. Remove any flowers or buds and the bottom leaves from each cutting.

**2** Dip the cut ends in rooting powder, tap off any excess, and insert the cuttings in pots of moist, soilless potting mix.

**3** Place a plastic bag over each pot to maintain a humid atmosphere. Support the bag with stakes to hold it away from the cutting. Place in a warm place out of direct sunlight. Check daily and ventilate if moisture builds up inside the bag.

**4** After a month, tug gently—if the plant resists, this means that roots have formed. Rooting can take up to two months.

**5** After roots form, remove the bag. Put the pot outdoors to acclimate for a few days, then transplant. If winter is near, keep young plants in pots until spring in a protected cold frame or a greenhouse.

# 'FRAU DAGMAR HARTOPP'
## Shrub (Hybrid Rugosa)

**Zones:** 3–8

**Size:** 2–4 ft. tall, 4 ft. wide

**Bloom Time:** Early to midsummer, repeat

**Bloom Width:** 3 in.

**Fragrance:** Strong

**Thorniness:** Very

Unlike many roses, 'Frau Dagmar Hartopp' ends the growing season with a bang. Its dark green, shiny, deeply veined leaves turn deep reddish purple, then change to rich gold. Large, gleaming, orange-red hips bring color to the garden in fall, when they take the place of faded flowers. The plant is small for a rugosa, and it may eventually grow wider than tall. Thorns in many lengths cover the entire cane. The flowers are intensely fragrant with the scent of cloves, and each has five light pink petals that form a saucer around creamy stamens. The first bloom comes in early to midseason, and repeats until frost. A Danish hybrid introduced around 1914, 'Frau Dagmar Hartopp' is very winter hardy. (It is sometimes offered as 'Frau Dagmar Hastrup'.)

## HOW TO GROW

Like other hybrid rugosas, this rose thrives in hot, dry conditions. It excels in problem areas where gentler plants may falter. Any spot in full sun with well-drained soil will do. Prune in late winter or early spring while plants are still dormant. Remove any dead or damaged canes and one or two of the oldest, thickest stems. Prune back the remaining canes by one-third. While the foliage is tough and disease resistant, rose stem girdler causes canes to swell and die. Control by removing infested canes as soon as they appear. Handpick Japanese beetles if they pose a problem.

## HOW TO USE

'Frau Dagmar Hartopp' is excellent sited near south-facing walls or beside a driveway where heat is reflected. Because it tolerates salt, it's a good choice for beach houses and gardens near heavily salted roads. Its low, thick, spreading habit and very thorny canes make it an excellent candidate for a short, impenetrable hedge. Space plants 2½ to 3 feet apart for a hedge or group planting. It also makes a handsome addition to a mixed border or can stand on its own.

## Top Choice

• 'Yellow Frau Dagmar Hartopp', a hybrid rugosa, is not a sport of the pink 'Frau Dagmar Hartopp'; it's another name for 'Topaz Jewel'. Introduced in 1987, 'Topaz Jewel' is a larger plant and bears double, yellow, fruit-scented flowers with blooms all season long.

## COLLECTING ROSE SEEDS

Roses are no more difficult to raise from seeds than any number of other plants. Be advised, however, that unless you collect hips from a species rose, the result of your propagation project will be a plant unlike the one you got it from.

❶ Clip the hips from the plant when they are ripe, i.e., after several frosts but certainly before they have begun to shrivel.

❷ Shell the hips and dump the pulp in a fine-mesh strainer. Working under running water in the sink, pick out and rinse off all the seeds you can. A single rose hip may contain anywhere from one to nearly a hundred seeds.

❸ Sow the seeds in soilless mix and put the flats outdoors or in the refrigerator so they get the cold treatment they need to break the seed dormancy.

# 'GRAHAM THOMAS'
## Shrub (English)

Zones: 5–9

Size: 4–8 ft. tall,
4–5 ft. wide

Bloom Time: Summer,
with variable repeat

Bloom Width: 3–4 in.

Fragrance: Strong

Thorniness: Moderate

The renowned English rosarian Graham Thomas chose this plant, introduced by David Austin in 1983, to bear his name. The flowers are an unforgettable rich golden yellow, full, and fragrant. Each bloom has thirty-five petals that retain the blossom's signature cupped shape until they fall. Austin described its tea-rose fragrance as slightly tarry, like the leaves of China tea. The deliciously pungent scent can suffuse a warm room.

### HOW TO GROW

Give this beauty full sun and well-drained, rich soil generously amended with rotted manure or organic matter. Add a layer of mulch at planting time and renew every spring and fall. Fertilize with a complete rose fertilizer in spring when the new leaves begin to emerge and again after the first flush of flowers. In late winter or early spring, cut the canes back by one-half to two-thirds. Prune again after the first bloom has faded to encourage rebloom. Trim any long canes that develop in late summer to keep the shrub well shaped. To control black spot, apply fungicidal soap when leaves emerge in spring and reapply as needed throughout the season. In Zone 5, the limit of its range, mound a 12-inch layer of soil over the base of the plant to protect it from winter damage.

### HOW TO USE

'Graham Thomas' has a tall, narrow, upright habit. If you live in an area with a long growing season, pruning the canes back hard (see above) may keep the plant shorter and the blooms lower on the stems. One bush makes an excellent addition to the mixed border, where its yellow, peony-like blooms can be appreciated with herbaceous perennials. Since much of this plant's energy goes into producing flowers and not into creating a dense shrub, a group planting creates a fuller look.

## Top Choices

- Lovely 'Heritage', released by Austin in 1984, has cupped, soft pink flowers, a strong, sweet fragrance, and (like 'Graham Thomas') foliage that is not very dense. 'Perdita', a descendant of 'Heritage', has light pink flowers flushed with yellow and a spicy aroma.

- 'Charlotte' is a butter yellow sport of 'Graham Thomas' introduced by Austin in 1993.

## ROSES IN CONTAINERS

Potted roses add life and color to a deck, balcony, or patio. Their roots need plenty of room, so you must work with large containers (at least 18 inches wide and deep). Locate pots in ample sunlight.

- For good drainage, start with a soilless potting mix in a selected container.

- Even roses in large pots with plenty of room for roots may chafe at confinement. Trim often to keep in bounds. Think twice before adding other plants to the same pot—the subterranean competition can be fierce.

- Pots dry out quickly, so water frequently or rig with an automatic watering system. Feed regularly; containerized soil quickly runs out of nutrition, becoming only an anchor for the roots. Deadhead daily to keep the shrub looking its best.

- Potted roses are vulnerable to winter cold. When growth slows in fall, withhold fertilizer and cut back on water; mulch the soil surface. For added protection, wrap wire in a cylinder around the pot and stuff with raked leaves. (Or sink the plant into a protected location in the garden for winter.) Remove the covering (or retrieve from the garden) when you are sure spring has arrived.

# 'MARY ROSE'
## Shrub (English)

**Zones:** 5–9

**Size:** 4 ft. tall, 4 ft. wide

**Bloom Time:** Early summer to frost

**Bloom Width:** 4 in.

**Fragrance:** Moderate

**Thorniness:** Very

'Mary Rose', a 1983 David Austin introduction, looks like an old-fashioned charmer. Its compact, shrubby habit has an attractive fullness. Its loosely cupped rose-pink flowers recall treasured blooms of the past, and it has a pleasing, light anise fragrance. Yet unlike many old garden roses that bloom once a year in June, 'Mary Rose' blooms in early summer and repeats until frost. Its flowers are clustered on upright stems, and its leaves are large, shiny, and medium green. Vigorous, thorny canes take well to hard pruning or may be left long to form a bigger bush. 'Mary Rose' is also disease resistant and winter hardy.

### HOW TO GROW
'Mary Rose' thrives in full sun in well-drained soil amended with lots of organic matter. Fertilize with a

complete rose fertilizer in spring as buds begin to break and again after the first blooms begin to fade. In addition to routine pruning, deadhead (see page 61) to encourage repeat in late summer. 'Mary Rose' is more resistant to black spot than some other English roses, but the disease can appear during hot, humid summers. To control, apply fungicidal soap in spring as new leaves emerge. Reapply as needed throughout the growing season.

## HOW TO USE

If you covet the grace and allure of old garden roses but lack the space for one, compact 'Mary Rose' may be the answer. Because of its width, this rose is also suitable for planting side by side to form a low, thorny hedge. 'Mary Rose' makes a handsome container planting on a patio or near a door, where its sweet, delicate fragrance can be appreciated. Plant one 'Mary Rose' in a mixed border of shrubs and flowers, or create the effect of a large mound in the landscape by cultivating it in a group of three.

## Top Choices

- 'Winchester Cathedral' is a white sport, 'Redoute' is a light pink sport, and 'Striped Mary Rose' is pink and white. In all other respects, these English roses are identical to 'Mary Rose'.

## POTATO STARCH REMEDY

If you are desperately trying to control aphids, spider mites, and thrips but have had no success, douse the pests in a homemade concoction of potato starch. The thick, heavy mixture is inexpensive and easy to make. It acts by trapping the insects and eventually suffocating them.

**1** Mix 1 cup of potato starch powder with 1 gallon of water in a spray can.

**2** Add to the mixture a tablespoon of liquid soap (this helps it stick).

**3** Spray onto the foliage of your plants. Let it sit for a few days, but then be sure to wash it off with water before it harms the plants' photosynthesis.

## 'MARY ROSE' COMPANIONS

The intense, rosy pink hue of 'Mary Rose' looks fabulous in the company of blue to purple flowers such as catmint, lavender, veronica, and delphinium.

# 'MORDEN CENTENNIAL'
## Shrub

Zones: 3–9

Size: 3–4 ft. tall, 3 ft. wide

Bloom Time: Mid-season, good repeat

Bloom Width: 3–4 in.

Fragrance: Slight

Thorniness: Moderate

Gardeners in very cold climates will appreciate 'Morden Centennial'. This rugged rose survives temperatures down to -40°F. In summer it blooms prolifically, bearing lovely, fully double, medium pink blossoms. The cup-shaped, fifty-petaled flowers are lightly fragrant and are borne in clusters of up to fifteen. 'Morden Centennial' has an upright, bushy habit with semiglossy foliage. Its moderate disease resistance combined with plentiful midseason bloom and good repeat make it an excellent choice for gardens of the North. Introduced in 1980, 'Morden Centennial' was developed at the Morden, Manitoba, research station of the Canadian Department of Agriculture. Like the other roses in Morden's Parkland series, it is drought resistant enough to survive on Canada's semi-arid western plains.

## HOW TO GROW

This tough rose thrives in a range of soils so long as they are well drained. Like other Morden roses, it prefers a site in full sun. Fertilize in spring as new leaves are emerging with a complete rose fertilizer. Prune in late winter or early spring, cutting back the canes by one-third to one-half to encourage heavy flowering and vigorous growth. 'Morden Centennial' is resistant to many pests and diseases, including black spot.

## HOW TO USE

'Morden Centennial' is a hardy shrub rose, perfect for gardens with cold, windy winters. Because of its habit and a season of bloom that stretches almost eleven weeks, you can use it for a bushy, colorful, informal hedge. You can also mass it in a bed for a colorful focal point or use it in a mixed border with hardy perennials that have silvery foliage.

## Top Choice

- 'Morden Blush', introduced in 1988, is another entry in the Parkland series. This shrub bears light pink, slightly fragrant, fifty-petaled flowers and blooms for about twelve weeks. It stands about 2 feet tall, making it a solid choice for gardens with limited space. Zones 3 to 9.

## Taylor's Tips

### HARDEN OFF BEFORE WINTER

In cold climates, any soft new growth that exists on a plant in late fall will be injured by winter weather. Prevent this by convincing the tender growth to become hard and woody. Stop fertilizing after early summer (you can still spread compost). Reduce the amount of water you give the plants, starting four weeks before the first fall frost. Last but not least, if you've been deadheading, stop so that the plant can begin to form hips; this process naturally alerts a rosebush to begin slowing down.

### BAREROOT PLANTING

When you get a bareroot rose home, remove its wrapper and any packing material. Then groom it a bit to give it a more vigorous start. Cut off any dead-looking roots and canes, and trim back damaged ones. If the nursery hasn't already done so, cut back the top of the plant to no fewer than three sturdy branches from the base, about 5 inches long. Finally, soak the plant in a bucket or tub of water to rehydrate it, overnight or for up to 24 hours.

# 'PENELOPE'
## Shrub (Hybrid Musk)

Zones: 6–9

Size: 5–7 ft. tall,
5–6 ft. wide

Bloom Time: Mid-
season bloom, good
repeat, excellent in fall

Bloom Width: 3 in.

Fragrance: Strong

Thorniness: Moderate

Powerfully fragrant, creamy flowers flushed pale coral-pink make 'Penelope' a charming garden addition. A hybrid musk rose introduced in 1924, 'Penelope' has orange-pink buds that fade to blush as they open. The semidouble blooms have eighteen to twenty-four petals and showy golden stamens. Flowers have a strong musky fragrance. Although individual blossoms grow white as they fade, the overall color effect of the shrub is palest pink. They appear in large and small clusters and are followed in fall by unusual, long-lasting hips that start out green and slowly turn a delicate coral-pink. This large, vigorous shrub blooms heavily in mid-season and fall but has a reliable repeat all summer long. 'Penelope' has a dense, bushy, upright habit with thorny canes and medium green, semiglossy leaves.

## HOW TO GROW

'Penelope' prefers full sun to light afternoon shade. Plant in well-drained, organically rich soil. Fertilize in spring and again after the first flush of flowers has faded with a complete rose fertilizer. Prune in spring before new growth begins; remove dead and damaged canes and cut back remaining stems by one-quarter to one-third of their length. 'Penelope' is resistant to pests and diseases but can get black spot and powdery mildew if weather conditions favor these diseases. To control, apply fungicidal soap in spring as new leaves emerge. Repeat as needed throughout the growing season. Rake and remove dead leaves from around the plant in fall.

## HOW TO USE

Because of its size, vigor, and continual blooms, 'Penelope' makes an excellent hedge. You can also grow it massed in beds. It, too, makes a fine addition to the mixed border and can stand on its own as a garden specimen. But however you decide to grow this rose, keep it where you can smell its luxurious fragrance and see its extraordinary yet subtly colored hips.

## Top Choice

- 'Lavender Lassie' is another lovely hybrid musk. It was introduced in 1960 and has the signature musky fragrance, but with brighter color than 'Penelope'—it's a sweet lavender-pink.

## GRAFTED VS. OWN-ROOT ROSES

In the nursery trade these days, the majority of roses seem to be grafted ones. Grafting is a fast and efficient way to propagate more roses as well as to quickly introduce new varieties. Raising roses on their own roots, on the other hand, is a slower process, but advocates feel the plants are worth the wait.

Grafted plants allow a rose that might naturally have a weak root system to use the more hardy, vigorous system of its surrogate. The rootstock may also confer disease or pest resistance, though some have spread a debilitating virus; make sure your supplier states that stock is "certified virus-free." The only drawback you may notice is an occasional sucker emerging from below the graft. You should cut it off, because it won't be the same, nor indeed as attractive, as the rest of the bush.

Gardeners in very cold climates (Zone 4 and north) are better off with own-root roses. Extremely cold winter temperatures tend to kill the aboveground portion but will spare the rootstock, which can send out new growth from the base when spring returns. Fans of own-root roses also say that the plants are longer lived.

# 'SALLY HOLMES'
## Shrub

**Zones:** 5–9

**Size:** 5–12 ft. tall, 5–6 ft. wide

**Bloom Time:** All summer

**Bloom Width:** 3 in.

**Fragrance:** Slight

**Thorniness:** Moderate

The vigor of its canes and the abundance of single blooms in its flower clusters make 'Sally Holmes' a memorable plant. The buff-colored buds open to creamy white, five-petaled blooms with showy golden stamens. The slightly fragrant blooms appear in huge clusters of up to sixty. 'Sally Holmes' blooms all summer long and stands tall, though with a somewhat lazy, sprawling habit. Glossy green, leathery leaves cover this hale and bushy plant. Introduced in 1976, 'Sally Holmes' is disease resistant.

### HOW TO GROW
'Sally Holmes' prefers a site in full sun, but it can also grow in areas that provide an hour or two of light shade. Give this rose organically rich soil, and fertilize with a complete rose fertilizer when leaves begin to

emerge in spring. Prune in late winter or early spring when the plants are still dormant. Remove thin or crowded canes as well as old or damaged ones. 'Sally Holmes' may get black spot; apply a preventative spray of fungicidal soap as leaves emerge in spring. If Japanese beetles are a problem, handpick to remove them.

### HOW TO USE

Its size, vigor, and abundance of continual blooms make 'Sally Holmes' an excellent rose for a large garden. Use it as a specimen or to add color all season to a large shrub border. Because some canes may reach a height of 12 feet, it can also be trained as a climber.

## Top Choices

- 'Ballerina', introduced in 1937, has great clusters of single flowers, albeit smaller than those of 'Sally Holmes', with white centers and deep pink rims. It has a light, musky fragrance. Growing 3 to 4 feet tall, it has an arching habit, shaped like a ballerina's skirt, which gave the plant its name.

- 'Rosy Carpet' also grows about 3 feet tall and somewhat wider. It produces abundant clusters of 1-inch, fragrant blooms in a deep shade of pink and repeats in fall.

## FOR BEAUTIFUL BOUQUETS

**1** Harvest long rose stems in the garden, placing them gently in an empty basket or bucket. If you cut unopened buds, make sure their sepals are peeling back and that they are poised to burst open. (For advice on how to make a proper cut, see "Deadheading," page 61.)

**2** Once indoors, recut each stem underwater. This prevents air bubbles, the reason for failed blossoms.

**3** Put some floral preservative in a vase or bucket and fill with very hot water. Stir to dissolve.

**4** Set freshly cut stems in the water and allow water to return to room temperature so the roses absorb the preservative.

**5** When the water is cool, move the bucket to a dark, cool place (such as a closet or cupboard) for a few hours or overnight.

**6** Arrange and display your beautiful roses with pride!

# 'SEA FOAM'
## Shrub

Zones: 4–9

Size: 2–3 ft. tall,
7 ft. wide

Bloom Time: Mid-
season, with excellent
repeat

Bloom Width: 2 in.

Fragrance: Slight

Thorniness: Moderate

This is an easy rose to love. 'Sea Foam' is remarkably practical with long, vigorous canes that quickly spread out to give dense coverage to an area up to 6 feet wide. When the slightly fragrant blossoms open, they are tinged with a pale pink that turns to a rich, creamy white. The plant bears sprays of medium-sized, double flowers with thirty to thirty-five petals that stand out against the small, dark green, glossy leaves. Grown as a ground cover, 'Sea Foam' measures 3 feet high and sprawls outward. The entire plant is exceptionally disease resistant and winter hardy.

### HOW TO GROW

Site this rose in full sun in organically rich soil. When massing for a hedge or ground cover effect, set plants

3½ to 4 feet apart. Fertilize with a complete rose food as new leaves emerge in spring. Prune 'Sea Foam' in late winter or early spring, removing the oldest canes to restore vigor and increase flower production. This rose can develop black spot during warm, wet summers. To control, apply a fungicidal soap or sulfur as new leaves emerge, then as needed throughout summer. Remove any Japanese beetles by hand as they appear.

### HOW TO USE

The long, trailing canes and vigorous growth of 'Sea Foam' make it a superb ground cover grown on flat areas and drifting down inclines, where its lazy habit looks particularly attractive. It can also be trained upright as a rambler or climber against a low wall or fence. In addition, 'Sea Foam' makes an effective massed planting or a handsome low hedge.

## Top Choices

- 'White Dawn', a parent of 'Sea Foam', climbs to a height of 12 feet and grows up to 8 feet wide. It bears pure white, fragrant, semidouble blossoms that flower early and repeat in late summer.

- 'Francine Austin', an English rose bred by David Austin in 1988, is slightly taller than 'Sea Foam' and almost as wide. Its abundant clusters of snow white pompoms have the added advantage of sweet fragrance.

## DETERMINING SOIL TEXTURE

Soils are divided into three distinct textures: light, medium, and heavy. Fortunately, each type of soil will support the growth of roses. Even so, it is helpful to know what kind of soil you have and how it will affect rose health.

- Light soil has a high concentration of sand and very efficient drainage. Roses grown in light soil need frequent watering and feeding. Improve this type of soil by digging in organic material, not just the first season but topdressing every year.

- Medium soil is the easiest to work with. It will produce healthy roses, assuming you provide adequate water, food, and occasional topdressing.

- Heavy soil is clay based, dense, and sticky. Surprisingly, heavy soil has the reputation of growing the best roses. Roses grown in this soil, however, require constant attention to prevent compaction so roots can breathe and water can penetrate. Do plenty of soil loosening before planting your rose. Lighten the soil by adding vermiculite or pumice as well as lots of compost or other organic matter. It takes time for a young rose to establish itself in heavy soil.

# 'THE FAIRY'
## Shrub (Polyantha)

**Zones:** 4–9

**Size:** 3–4 ft. tall, 4 ft. wide

**Bloom Time:** Summer, excellent repeat

**Bloom Width:** 1 in.

**Fragrance:** None

**Thorniness:** Moderate

If you're looking for a rose that's practically guaranteed to thrive, try 'The Fairy', a favorite with gardeners since its introduction in 1932. Although this rose looks pretty and delicate, it's actually tough, disease resistant, and hardy to about -35°F without protection. The cupped, light pink flowers are small and cover the plant throughout summer and into fall. Each double blossom has twenty-four to thirty petals and grows in large flower clusters that, when cut, make handsome bouquets, though with little to no scent. The habit of 'The Fairy' is compact, tidy, and somewhat arching. Tiny, glossy, bright green leaves cloak its moderately thorny canes. This versatile rose can also be grown as a standard for use in small gardens, to flank an entry, or as a focal point.

## HOW TO GROW

'The Fairy' grows and flowers best in full sun but does tolerate some light shade. Plant in a well-drained soil amended with some organic matter. Use a complete rose fertilizer in spring after plants have been pruned. In late winter while plants are dormant, remove one or two of the oldest canes; trim remaining stems back by about one-quarter. 'The Fairy' may get some black spot or powdery mildew in some years. To control, apply a fungicidal soap in spring as new leaves emerge, then repeat as required.

## HOW TO USE

Because of its neat habit and continual bloom, 'The Fairy' does well in pots, at the front of the border, or in small gardens with limited space. It makes an attractive ever-blooming hedge and an effective focal point when massed in the landscape. The compact habit and delicate flowers and foliage of 'The Fairy' complement perennials such as salvias and lamb's-ears.

## *Top Choices*

- 'Lovely Fairy' is similar in all respects to the original, but it has much darker pink flowers; in cool weather, they may even tend to light red.

- 'Surrey', of which 'The Fairy' is a parent, was introduced in England in 1987 and is said to be ideal as a ground cover rose because it grows thickly and spreads widely. It has a light fragrance.

- 'The Fairy, Climbing' is a sport of 'The Fairy' that grows 8 to 12 feet high.

## BUTTERFLY SCREENS

Although roses don't attract as many butterflies as other plants, they can serve a beneficial role in a butterfly garden. As a rule, butterflies are not fond of windy sites. If the only location available to you is routinely buffeted by a prevailing breeze, a windscreen is in order.

Evergreens and deciduous trees create an ideal barrier, but a complement of rose shrubs is even more effective. The dense, low foliage will soften the wind. As a bonus, a rose barrier also gives birds and other wildlife a food source and a place to nest.

## POLYANTHA'S PAST

Hardy and easy to grow, polyantha roses were developed in France late in the nineteenth century. They are a natural cross between China roses, which are continual bloomers, and multifloras, which bear flowers in large sprays or clusters.

# 'WILLIAM BAFFIN'
## Shrub

Zones: 3–9

Size: 8–12 ft. tall, 6 ft. wide

Bloom Time: Mid-season, excellent repeat

Bloom Width: 3–4 in.

Fragrance: None

Thorniness: Moderate

'William Baffin', one of the hardiest modern roses, is really two kinds of rose in one. You can grow this rose, known for vigor and disease resistance, as a dense, upright, somewhat arching shrub, or you can train it as a climber. It bears deep pink, semidouble, twenty-petaled flowers that grow in clusters of up to thirty. When fully open, the blossoms display vivid yellow stamens. The first flush of bloom occurs in mid-season, and flowering repeats fairly well through early fall. Deadhead spent flowers to encourage continued flowering. While 'William Baffin' is not a prolific bloomer, it is hardy to temperatures down to -40°F and is pest- and disease-free. In particular, it is fully resistant to black spot, mildew, and rust—a plus in humid climates. Glossy, bright green leaves cover the long canes. Introduced in 1983 and named after a Canadian explorer, 'William Baffin' was developed at the Canadian Department of Agriculture's Central Experimental Farm in Ottawa, Ontario. Like other roses in the Explorer series, 'William Baffin' is ideal for gardens in the coldest climates.

## HOW TO GROW

'William Baffin' needs full sun and does best in well-worked soil to which some organic matter has been added. Fertilize after pruning in spring and in early summer. When grown as a climber, train the canes to a lateral support such as a rail fence for best flowering. When grown as a free-flowing shrub, allow the canes to arch to the ground for the heaviest flowering.

## HOW TO USE

'William Baffin' is perfect for gardens with cold winters and humid summers. Because of its upright habit and long bloom period, it works well as a tall hedge. It also makes an excellent climber if its tough canes are trained to a trellis or fence.

## Top Choices

- 'Henry Kelsey' bears bright red, fragrant, twenty-five-petaled flowers with gold stamens in clusters of ten to fifteen. Use this vigorous 8-foot-tall shrub, which blooms for nine weeks, as a low arching bush or as a climber. Zones 3 to 9.

- 'John Cabot' has glowing red flowers with forty petals and blooms for over ten weeks. It can be grown as an 8-foot-tall shrub or a climber. Zones 3 to 9.

## Taylor's Tips

### DRIP IRRIGATION

One way to conserve water and lessen your workload is to install a drip irrigation system in your garden, which you can purchase at a garden supply store or through a mail-order catalog. It consists of hose lines and emitters that water plants at their base, drop by drop.

Drip irrigation is good tack for roses, because it keeps water off the leaves. (Wet foliage leads to disease.) Also, liquid fertilizers can be applied through the drip system with the water. If you feel daunted by installation, hire a professional to put the system in place.

### THE DISTINGUISHED EXPLORER SERIES

*R. x kordesii,* a species discovered by German plantsman Wilhelm Kordes and introduced in 1953, is a parent of many roses in the Explorer series, including 'William Baffin', 'Henry Kelsey', and 'John Cabot'. Among the valued traits of *R. x kordesii* are outstanding cold hardiness and a medium-sized climbing habit.

# APOTHECARY ROSE
## Old Garden Rose (*R. gallica officinalis*)

**Zones:** 4–8

**Size:** 3 ft. tall,
4 ft. wide

**Bloom Time:** Mid-
season, with no repeat

**Bloom Width:** 3 in.

**Fragrance:** Moderate

**Thorniness:** Very

Gardeners grow the apothecary rose not only for use in crafts, cooking, medicines, and potpourris (the scent of the petals intensifies after drying) but also for its simple beauty. Deep pink, cupped flowers are semi-double with twelve to eighteen petals and attractive gold stamens; they appear in profusion in early summer. Red hips follow. The habit is mounded, upright, and compact with bristly canes and rough, grayish green leaves. This rose is both disease resistant and winter hardy, requiring a period of winter dormancy to flower well.

### HOW TO GROW
This rose prefers a site in full sun but will tolerate a little shade. It will also tolerate less-than-perfect soil conditions, but it does best in fertile ground with good

drainage. In early summer, after flowering is over, trim back stems to remove spent flower heads (unless you want hips) and remove any weak canes. It is resistant to many diseases but sometimes gets powdery mildew in late summer. This is usually not a serious problem. To control, rake up and discard dead leaves in fall.

### How to Use

Apothecary rose is perfect as a colorful feature in (or framing) an herb garden. It is an excellent specimen plant because of the glowing flower color and rich, spicy fragrance. In the mixed border, its powerful color again becomes an asset, particularly when serving as a complement to other hot garden colors. It also makes a casual, low-maintenance hedge that can be shaped right after blooming.

## Top Choices

- *R. gallica versicolor* 'Rosa Mundi' is an ancient sport of the apothecary rose, with semidouble, spicily fragrant petals that are striped and speckled red on pink. Otherwise, this shrub is remarkably similar to the original, with a 3-foot height and 3-inch blooms.

- 'The Herbalist' is a recently introduced David Austin English rose that looks very similar to the apothecary rose but offers repeat blooms.

## Drying Rose Petals

Dried rose petals are wonderful in homemade potpourris and sachets, either alone or combined with other dried flowers or herbs. Here's how to dry them for maximum color and fragrance:

**1** Harvest roses just as the flowers begin to open. Early in the morning is best, after the dew has had a chance to dry but before the hot sun evaporates the plant's fragrant oils.

**2** Pull the petals from the flowers and spread them out in a single layer on a screen.

**3** Set the screen with petals in a dark, well-ventilated place to dry.

**4** When dry, store the petals in an airtight glass container out of bright light until you are ready to use them.

# 'CELESTIAL'
## Old Garden Rose (Alba)

Zones: 3–9

Size: 5 ft. tall, 5 ft. wide

Bloom Time: Early, with no repeat

Bloom Width: 3 in.

Fragrance: Strong

Thorniness: Slight

This rose belongs to the category of old roses known as the albas. As the name implies, these bear white (or pale pink), richly scented flowers that are set against a backdrop of grayish green foliage. The blush pink blossoms of 'Celestial' are cupped, with twenty to twenty-five petals set in an even, circular arrangement. When fully open, a delicate, central tuft of gold stamens is apparent. A Dutch hybrid from the end of the eighteenth century, it has an upright, bushy habit and surprisingly few thorns. Its soft-colored leaves are an elegant contrast to the delicate blush of the blossoms and look particularly handsome against the dark green foliage of other plants. 'Celestial', also known as 'Celeste', can handle cold winters.

## HOW TO GROW

'Celestial' grows best in fertile, loamy soil with good drainage and plenty of water, though it adapts to less-than-ideal conditions. It prefers full sun but will tolerate part shade. It needs little pruning beyond removing dead or damaged canes in spring. If desired, the plants can be lightly trimmed to shape. It is not troubled by pests or diseases.

## HOW TO USE

In spite of its charming flowers, 'Celestial' is a tough plant that can grow in adverse conditions. You can use it in hedges, in borders, as an elegant specimen, or even trained on an east-facing wall or fence (it tolerates some shade). 'Celestial' also works well as a transitional plant, easing the contrast between a formal area close to the house and an informally landscaped area beyond.

## Top Choice

- *R.* x *alba* 'Semi-plena', at least as ancient as 'Celestial', is an upright shrub that stands somewhat taller (6 to 7 feet) with white, intensely fragrant, almost single flowers. It, too, blooms only once early in the season.

## PLANTING AN ISLAND BED

When you run out of space in your gardens and flower beds, you can still plant additional roses. With some creative landscaping, you can go in a new direction by forming island beds. Not only will an island bed allow you to grow more roses, it will also add height to a flat yard and provide a break in an expansive lawn.

❶ The shape and composition of an island bed should mirror your other flower borders. Take a good look at surrounding borders and get a sense of the key elements that you would like to carry over into the island bed.

❷ Site tall plants in the middle of the garden with progressively shorter plants toward the exterior of the bed, so it will be attractive from all sides. If the biggest plant is a once-blooming rose such as 'Celestial', plant some later-blooming perennials so there will always be something blooming in the bed.

❸ Add a brick or stone edging to help maintain the shape of the bed. Alternatively, purchase plastic edging to bury in the ground around the bed.

# 'CHARLES DE MILLS'

## Old Garden Rose (Gallica)

**Zones:** 4–8

**Size:** 4–5 ft. tall, 4 ft. wide

**Bloom Time:** Mid-season, with no repeat

**Bloom Width:** 3 in.

**Fragrance:** Slight

**Thorniness:** Moderate

The cupped magenta blooms of 'Charles de Mills', the largest-flowered gallica rose, are extraordinary for the number and organization of their petals. Numbering about two hundred, they are neatly packed and swirled in an arrangement that, when partly open, makes for a flower that is perfectly flat on top. Fully open, the blooms are ball shaped with a spot of light green deep in the center. Actual color may vary beyond magenta to crimson, wine, and violet. Blossoms are lightly scented and held high on their stalks. 'Charles de Mills', probably bred in Europe in the nineteenth century, is a shrub with thick, erect canes and some suckering. Canes may bend under the weight of the big flowers. Leaves are toothed, glossy, and dark green. 'Charles de Mills' is disease resistant and winter hardy.

## HOW TO GROW

Full sun is best. 'Charles de Mills' will, however, tolerate a few hours of light shade. It enjoys fertile soil and good drainage, but it will settle for slightly less if need be. Prune plants in late winter or early spring while still dormant. This rose can get powdery mildew late in the season; if so, apply fungicidal soap to the leaves.

## HOW TO USE

'Charles de Mills' makes an attractive hedge; prune to shape in late winter or early spring, or leave unpruned for an informal look. Planted in groups of three, it creates a bold impact in the landscape when in bloom, particularly because of the way it holds its big blooms aloft. Silver- or gray-leaved plants contrast with the richly colored flowers and dark leaves, while plants with red or purple flowers harmonize with its floral tones.

## Top Choice

- 'Cardinal de Richelieu' is another splendid gallica. Introduced in France in 1840, the purple of its double blooms is more consistently dark than 'Charles de Mills' (indeed, it is considered the darkest of the gallicas). The shrub is compact, measuring about 3 feet tall, with dark, somewhat shiny leaves and few thorns.

## USING GALLICAS AS GROUND COVER

As gardeners look for labor-saving ways to maintain their yards, they often turn to ground covers. The best ones need to be tough and hardy, while requiring a minimum of pruning and care.

Planted in masses, gallica roses make good ground covers for flat land or low banks because of their modest height, suckering habit, and tolerance of relatively poor soil conditions.

After planting, lay down a mulch at their bases to suppress weeds and retain soil moisture.

Remove dead and diseased branches each spring and prune stems back to help keep growth low and even.

## RECUTTING ROSES

You can extend the vase life of homegrown or purchased roses by recutting them after you bring them in the house. Fill a medium-sized bowl with water, submerge the stem end, and make a fresh cut underwater. This prevents air bubbles from entering and blocking the stem; it assures that roses in a vase will continue to take up water and therefore last longer.

# 'HARISON'S YELLOW'
## Old Garden Rose

Zones: 4–9

Size: 5–7 ft. tall,
3 ft. wide

Bloom Time: Early season, with no repeat

Bloom Width: 2 in.

Fragrance: Slight

Thorniness: Very

Introduced in New York in 1830, 'Harison's Yellow' quickly became an American staple. Tough and hardy, it bears small, clear yellow roses along thorny, reddish brown canes. The flowers are double and cupped with twenty to twenty-four petals. Frilly gold stamens add a delicate touch to the blooms, which have a light, sweet fragrance. The plant has attractive ferny foliage with toothed, medium green, rounded leaflets and an upright, arching, free-growing form. 'Harison's Yellow' is not a vigorous grower and starts off more slowly than many newer hybrid roses; be sure to select only strong, healthy-looking plants. However, once established, 'Harison's Yellow' is winter hardy and disease resistant. Pioneers, who considered this rose a prize possession, took it West with them. It became known as "the yellow rose of Texas" and inspired a popular ballad by the same name.

### How to Grow

Although 'Harison's Yellow' prefers a location in full sun, it will grow and flower well in part shade. It can grow in poor soil conditions and is drought tolerant, but prospers in fertile soil with good drainage. 'Harison's Yellow' is pest resistant and requires no spraying; occasionally you may have to remove diseased or dead canes.

### How to Use

Because of its drought and shade tolerance, 'Harison's Yellow' can grow where other roses would perish. It works well planted among bushier shrubs that complement its erect habit. Its informal habit lets it blend easily into wilder parts of the landscape, where its abundant yellow blooms will add welcome color. Though it blooms only once, its disease-resistant foliage makes it an asset next to or behind garden beds. Use it as a pleasing backdrop to bearded irises and peonies.

## Top Choice

- 'William's Double Yellow' comes from the same parents as 'Harison's Yellow'. A principal difference between the two flowers is the centers; this one has green carpels instead of the showy stamens found on 'Harison's Yellow'. It is also somewhat shorter (about 4 feet tall) and suckers profusely.

## THORNY ISSUES

Roses and thorns go hand in hand, and certainly poets and songwriters have made much of the "beauty-and-the-beast" nature of this pairing. Thorns do have constructive reasons for being. First, they protect the plant from predators (though hungry deer or cattle will eat from a prickly rosebush if desperate). They also prove useful to the plant for support—large or small, thorns help a rose clutch a fence, trellis, or tree. These qualities enhance survival, of course, which is why most roses are thorny.

Botanists do not consider rose thorns to be true thorns, because they are a product of the epidermal cells on the surface of the plant, rather than an outgrowth of the woody core beneath (like the thorns on a hawthorn tree, for instance). As a result, you can snap off rose thorns fairly easy with a flick of your thumb. Florists use a special tool called a "stem stripper" to remove the thorns as they zip it down the length of the rose's stem.

# 'KÖNIGIN VON DÄNEMARK'
## Old Garden Rose (Alba)

Zones: 3–9

Size: 5–6 ft. tall, 4–5 ft. wide

Bloom Time: Early, with no repeat

Bloom Width: 3 in.

Fragrance: Strong

Thorniness: Very

When a soft pink bloom of 'Königin von Dänemark' first opens, it looks cupped. As it ages, its two hundred or so petals unfurl and take on a quartered appearance, with the outer petals reflexing and almost paling to white. A green button center adds to the charm and beauty of this richly fragrant bloom. Powdery, dark blue-green foliage enhances the shrub's elegance, creating the perfect foil for its baby pink flowers. Introduced in 1826, 'Königin von Dänemark' is vigorous, tall for a shrub rose, with very thorny canes and an open form. It is particularly cold hardy.

### HOW TO GROW
'Königin von Dänemark' thrives in full sun, but unlike many old garden roses also grows and flowers well in part shade. It prefers a well-drained soil with lots of

well-rotted manure or other organic matter. Fertilize in spring with a complete granular rose fertilizer. In summer, apply a water-soluble fertilizer at one-half the label rate as the summer blooms are fading. Mulch in spring and again in fall to keep soil moist. As for pruning, take out one or two of the oldest canes each spring before new growth begins. This rose is not seriously troubled by pests or diseases.

### HOW TO USE

'Königin von Dänemark' makes an elegant, loose, informal hedge. The long canes can be trained to grow on a trellis to cover a wall. It also works well in a mixed border, where its flowers, foliage, and tree-like form can be appreciated.

## Top Choice

- 'Maiden's Blush', a hybrid alba introduced in the late sixteenth century, has slightly smaller and lighter-colored blooms. They are a luscious, light pink, extremely full and fragrant, but lack button centers. This shrub blooms profusely from early to midseason and does not repeat. It has a more arching profile.

## USING SULFUR WISELY

Sulfur can be a lifesaver in your rose garden. Its properties are effective at controlling fungal spores from germinating (thus helping prevent rust and mildew), and it also kills spider mites.

- Sulfur will only help your plants if it is present on the leaves before disease spores arrive. It must be applied repeatedly, especially after heavy rains.

- Sulfur comes powdered (for dusting) and as a liquid (for spraying). Both are effective, but the liquid form is easier to apply.

- Never use sulfur when it is very warm out. In temperatures hotter than 80°F, sulfur will burn your plants.

## NOURISHING REPEAT BLOOMERS

Old garden roses that bloom only once a year can tolerate poorer growing conditions than roses that repeat bloom. Roses that bloom continuously require richer soil, more water and sunlight, and frequent fertilizing to look their best and to keep their flowers coming.

# 'MADAME HARDY'
## Old Garden Rose (Damask)

**Zones:** 4–9

**Size:** 5–6 ft. tall, 5 ft. wide

**Bloom Time:** Mid-season, with no repeat

**Bloom Width:** 3 in.

**Fragrance:** Moderate

**Thorniness:** Moderate

Take the fullness and beauty of the classic old-rose form, add a sweet musky fragrance touched with lemon, color the resulting flower white, and you have 'Madame Hardy', a hybrid damask rose. Showy sepals encase the fat pink buds. They open into blooms that are at first cupped, then flat, and finally curved backward. Flowers, which grow in clusters, have roughly two hundred petals, so the effect is quite lush. Their neat, balanced arrangement includes a central frill of little white petals surrounding a green pip. 'Madame Hardy' has ample, downy, light green leaves on moderately thorny canes. Its habit is upright and bushy, and it is both winter hardy and fairly disease resistant.

## HOW TO GROW

Give this rose a spot in full sun, in well-drained soil that has been amended with plenty of organic matter. Once established, add a 2-inch-deep layer of rotted manure or compost in spring and again in fall. Use a complete rose fertilizer once in spring as growth begins and again after flowering is complete. After the flowers fade, shorten the canes by one-quarter to one-third their length. 'Madame Hardy' is moderately susceptible to black spot, with symptoms of the disease appearing most frequently in late summer. To control, apply a fungicidal soap in spring as leaves emerge and again throughout the season as necessary.

## HOW TO USE

'Madame Hardy' makes a lovely, tall hedge. Its perfectly formed, aromatic flowers are also a superb addition to a cutting garden. The blooms look elegant in mixed borders with plants of equal merit and equally delicate hue.

## *Top Choice*

- 'Ispahan', a damask rose from Iran, has free-flowering clusters of intensely fragrant, double, medium pink flowers that bloom for almost two months at the beginning of summer—longer than most other damasks. It, too, is a large shrub about 5 feet tall and wide.

## DEADHEADING: PRECISION COUNTS

Pruning back fading flowers after a bush has bloomed is called "deadheading." This keeps your plant looking neat also it encourages more flowering and new growth. Otherwise, plants spend energy going to seed, that is, forming hips. Always use good, sharp pruners.

**1** Find the first pair of five-leaflet leaves below the spent flower. If there are several pairs of three-leaflet leaves below it, play it safe and cut above the second pair instead. (If you want your older roses to have longer stems for bouquets, you may cut the stem at the second five-leaflet leaf.)

**2** Cut about ¼ inch above the targeted spot, at a 45-degree angle pointing away from the center of the plant. Be precise, because a cut that is made too high will result in weak, thin new growth that is likely to fail.

**3** Stop deadheading a month before frost to help plants prepare for winter.

# 'STANWELL PERPETUAL'
## Old Garden Rose (Hybrid Spinosissima)

**Zones:** 3–8

**Size:** 3–5 ft. tall, 3–5 ft. wide

**Bloom Time:** Spring through fall

**Bloom Width:** 3 in.

**Fragrance:** Strong

**Thorniness:** Very

'Stanwell Perpetual' has been a garden favorite since its introduction in 1838. This tough, hardy rose is one of the earliest roses to start blooming and one of the last to stop. Blossoms are a translucent blush pink fading to white, with forty-five to fifty-five petals. They open slightly cupped but flatten with age, the outer petals curving backward. Their lush scent is sweet and spicy. The flower's muddled center gives it a charming look of informality. Once firmly established in the garden, 'Stanwell Perpetual' is the only hybrid spinosissima rose that offers reliable repeat bloom. This rose has very thorny canes and small, fernlike, dull green leaves. The bush is winter hardy and has excellent disease and pest resistance.

## HOW TO GROW

'Stanwell Perpetual' prefers a location in full sun for best flowering but also does well with a few hours of dappled shade. Grow it in well-drained soil to which rotted manure, compost, or other organic matter has been added, spacing plants 4 feet apart. After planting, add a layer of organic mulch around the root zone. Fertilize with a complete rose fertilizer in spring when growth begins. Prune 'Stanwell Perpetual' in late winter or early spring when plants are dormant. Remove dead or damaged canes and trim remaining canes to shape.

## HOW TO USE

The only drawback to this lovely garden rose is a somewhat spindly habit. The late renowned English garden designer Gertrude Jekyll admired 'Stanwell Perpetual' and recommended planting three bushes together about 1 foot apart to create the effect of one large, full shrub. Such a group can work in a mixed border or alone as a specimen. Once established, 'Stanwell Perpetual' also makes a fine, long-flowering hedge.

## Top Choice

- 'Frülingsmorgen' is a hybrid spinossima worthy of a place in any garden. In spring the dense, 5-foot-tall shrubs are covered with single flowers. The blossoms have a warm yellow center that fades to cool rose-pink at the edges of the petals. The plants are not repeat bloomers. Zones 4-9.

## Taylor's Tips

### SUCKER PATROL

If suckers appear from the rootstock below the bud union, remove them immediately. Untrimmed suckers sap valuable energy from a plant and, if it is grafted, produce foliage and flowers unlike (and less attractive than) the rest of the bush.

You will recognize a sucker by its long, thin growth and tiny leaves, which differ from those of the budded rose. Follow the sucker back to where it is attached to the main stem. Using pruners or the sharp edge of a trowel, cut it off.

### NO ENCORE, PLEASE

Avoid planting new roses in the same soil where other roses or shrubs have grown for a year or more. Roses and certain other shrubs are greedy feeders and the soil they grew in previously may be depleted. In addition, if you don't regularly rake out and dispose of fallen leaves, the ground and vegetation may be harboring pests and diseases. Either scrap the old soil and fill the hole with fresh new soil or plant the roses in a new location.

# 'TUSCANY SUPERB'
## Old Garden Rose (Gallica)

**Zones:** 4–8

**Size:** 3–4 ft. tall, 4 ft. wide

**Bloom Time:** Mid-season, with no repeat

**Bloom Width:** 4 in.

**Fragrance:** Strong

**Thorniness:** Moderate

'Tuscany Superb', a gallica rose, has large, fragrant blooms that are cupped, flat topped, and filled with velvety petals (between twenty-four and forty) the color of a dark wine or mulberry. Gold stamens add glowing contrast, though partly obscured by the ruffled effect of the inner petals. 'Tuscany Superb', probably bred in Europe in the nineteenth century, has thick, erect canes and suckering growth. With dark green leaves and plump, round buds, this rose makes an excellent garden specimen. It is both disease resistant and winter hardy, needing a period of winter dormancy to flower well.

### HOW TO GROW
'Tuscany Superb' will tolerate some shade and less-than-perfect soil conditions and still bloom, but its dark color

will lose its depth and fewer flowers will appear. It needs a site that offers fertile soil, good drainage, and plenty of water to perform its best. Pruning is minimal—after flowering is complete in summer, trim canes back by one-quarter. Occasionally black spot appears in late summer, but the disease does little damage. To control, rake up and discard fallen leaves in fall. Renew mulch around the base of the plant each spring and fall, and keep leaves as dry as possible in summer and fall.

### How to Use

'Tuscany Superb' makes an attractive hedge or landscape feature. Planted in groups of three, it creates a bold impact in the landscape when in bloom, particularly because 'Tuscany Superb' holds its big blooms aloft on strong stalks rather than letting them nod into the foliage. Planting 'Tuscany Superb' near shrubs with reddish leaves or red to purple flowers with a similar season of bloom brings out the depth and intensity of the rose's color.

## *Top Choice*

- 'Tuscany', commonly referred to as "The Old Velvet Rose," is the older, semidouble form of 'Tuscany Superb'. The flowers are similar but not as full, with eighteen to twenty-four petals. It is more compact, measuring 3 feet tall, with small, dark green leaves.

## WHAT IS ROSE VIRUS?

Some nurseries make a point of letting customers know that their plants are "virus-free" ("virus-indexed" or "rose mosaic virus-free"). They are referring to a chronic problem in the marketing of roses, particularly, it seems, in the United States—infected rootstocks.

The disease is passed in the fields where rose plants are grown commercially. It either moves from infected roots up into the budded stock, or down into a healthy rootstock when infected budded stock is grafted on. (It isn't passed by pruning shears or insects in the garden; one infected plant in your yard cannot give it to another.)

The first season or two, an affected rose may perform well, but then it begins to decline. Yellow streaking or a pale green, oak-leaf-like pattern may appear prominently on the leaves, not to be confused with normal chlorosis. In addition, there will be fewer blooms, and the rose may become too weak to survive a cold winter.

To make sure you are buying a virus-free rose, ask the nurseryman and/or examine the catalog for a guarantee. Note that own-root roses are usually virus-free, simply because they have no rootstock variety from which to catch the malady.

# 'ZÉPHIRINE DROUHIN'
## Old Garden Rose (Bourbon)

Zones: 6–9

Size: 8–12 ft. tall

Bloom Time: All season

Bloom Width: 4 in.

Fragrance: Strong

Thorniness: Slight

'Zéphirine Drouhin', a climbing Bourbon rose that dates back to 1868, produces cerise-pink blooms all season. The flowers are intensely fragrant, loosely cupped, and semidouble with twenty to twenty-four petals. Their vivid color stands out sharply against the semiglossy, medium green foliage, which is flushed with copper tones when new. 'Zéphirine Drouhin' is a vigorous, well-branched plant with long basal canes that are nearly thornless along with short-flowering latera canes. It is winter hardy only to Zone 6 and healthy, except for an occasional problem with mildew.

### HOW TO GROW
'Zéphirine Drouhin' requires full sun and organically rich soil in a location sheltered from winds. It can be grown either as a large, sprawling shrub or trained to

climb a support. As for pruning, before new growth begins each spring, remove a few of the oldest canes. Cut back remaining stems by up to half, leaving four or five vigorous buds per cane. Like most Bourbon roses, this one is susceptible to black spot. To control, apply fungicidal soap or garden sulfur to the new leaves in spring and repeat as needed throughout the growing season. Rake and dispose of dead leaves in fall.

### HOW TO USE

Because the canes of 'Zéphirine Drouhin' are mercifully smooth, you can plant it where you can appreciate both its looks and fragrance close up, such as adjacent to a walkway. You can also train it to climb a porch post, tree, or low wall. The long season of bloom (and few thorns) makes this a rewarding choice to flank a garden entrance. For large spaces, the bushes can be allowed to sprawl. Install a sturdy post on each side, or an arch, and train the two shrubs to grow vertically.

## Top Choices

- 'Kathleen Harrop' is a 1919 sport of 'Zéphirine Drouhin'. Its light pink flowers have a darker pink on the reverse of the petals, and it flowers continuously during the growing season. Its habit is similar, but the bush is less vigorous.

- 'Martha', a 1920s 'Zéphirine Drouhin' sport, has blooms of an even lighter pink with a hint of cream in the center.

## TESTING DRAINAGE

One factor that is important to the survival of all garden plants is soil drainage. Inadequate drainage will drown your plants, while too-fast drainage will carry away applied nutrients and eventually dehydrate even the hardiest of species. A simple test before planting will prevent heartache in the future.

**1** Dig a hole that is 1 to 2 feet deep and fill it with water. If the water is gone after 24 hours, your drainage will not be a problem.

**2** If the water is still in the hole after 24 hours, the drainage is poor and you should consider building a raised bed, embarking on a major double-digging project and adding in lightening agents (vast quantities of organic matter), or planting elsewhere.

**3** If you notice the water disappearing from the hole rapidly, you need to dig in some organic matter (shredded leaves, old manure, compost, grass clippings, etc.) to improve the soil's ability to hold moisture. Topdress annually with an inch of compost or other organic matter to help soil retain moisture.

# 'AMERICA'
## Climber

Zones: 5–9

Size: 9–12 ft. tall

Bloom Time: Mid-season to fall

Bloom Width: 4 in.

Fragrance: Strong

Thorniness: Moderate

Notable for its dependable, all-season bloom, 'America' is a large-flowered climber with double, coral-pink flowers. Each bloom has between forty and forty-five petals and a potent, spicy fragrance. Flowers begin high centered, but become cupped as they open. The habit of 'America' is upright, spreading, and vigorous, and the foliage is medium green and semiglossy. It blooms on old and new wood. The rose is tough, disease resistant, and winter hardy. 'America' was an All-America Rose Selection for 1976, a designation earned by few climbers.

### HOW TO GROW

'America' needs at least 6 hours of sun per day to thrive, if not more. Plant in well-drained soil amended with organic matter. Once a plant is three to four years old, begin removing a few of the oldest canes annually in early spring. Cut back remaining ones to four or five buds. 'America' can develop some black spot during wet, hot summers, and in the Pacific Northwest. Control with a fungicidal soap.

### HOW TO USE

'America' does well trained to grow up a trellis, wall, or arbor; just be sure to allow for some air circulation so it doesn't get mildew. (Install supports a few inches from a wall to allow air to circulate between the leaves and the wall.) Allowed to grow without support, the rose makes a sprawling hedge. Plant in groups to create a long-blooming mass of color in the landscape; a group makes a stunning cover for a large, sunny slope that you're tired of mowing.

## Top Choices

- 'Fragrant Cloud' is a parent of 'America', with coral-red flowers that are 5 inches wide and emit a more powerful, true-rose fragrance. A hybrid tea, it stands 5 feet tall and blooms all season long. 'Fragrant Cloud' has won prestigious awards in North America and Great Britain. It is winter hardy and disease resistant.

- 'Fragrant Cloud, Climbing' bears the same coral-red, richly scented blossoms as 'Fragrant Cloud', but with a climbing habit.

## WINTER PROTECTION FOR CLIMBERS

In regions where winter will likely bring on a hard frost and freezing temperatures, tender climbers need insulation from the elements to protect them from fluctuating temperatures and to prevent drying out.

**1** In late summer or early fall, start "hardening off" the climber by withholding fertilizer and gradually reducing water. Stop deadheading—this signals the plant to slow growth and start forming hips.

**2** Wrap the canes of the climber in burlap and secure with twine ties. Be sure to unwrap the canes as soon as spring arrives. Otherwise, the warmth inside the covering will cause the rose to put out new growth that will die when temperatures fluctuate.

**3** In areas where temperatures often drop below 10°F, your best bet is to bury the canes in the ground. Dig a trench, then carefully remove the canes from their support, loosely tie them together, and bury them with soil. Liberate the plant the following spring after all danger of frost is past.

# 'AMERICAN PILLAR'
## Rambler

Zones: 6–9

Size: 15–20 ft. tall

Bloom Time: Mid-season, with no repeat

Bloom Width: 2 in.

Fragrance: Slight to none

Thorniness: Moderate

This classic 1902 rambler is a generous bloomer, producing large sprays of bright, deep pink, single flowers with a white eye and gold stamens. Each small blossom has five petals. Birds enjoy the bright red hips that follow. The growth of 'American Pillar' is upright and vigorous. It produces long, moderately thorny canes and shiny, leathery, dark green leaves that turn purplish in fall. While in the South foliage is prone to mildew, plants are otherwise fairly resistant to diseases.

### HOW TO GROW

'American Pillar' prefers at least 6 hours of sun each day but can tolerate some shade. It flowers best in fertile soil with good drainage. Except for removing dead and injured wood, do not prune 'American Pillar' after planting or during the first two seasons of growth. Once established, remove weak or diseased shoots as needed. To increase the flowering shoots the following year, cut off the ends of the long canes. Alternatively, you can cut it back to the ground after flowering; the plant will produce new canes that will bloom the next year. In warm, dry conditions, 'American Pillar' can get some powdery mildew. To control, apply a fungicidal soap to the new leaves in spring and repeat as required.

## HOW TO USE

If allowed to sprawl, 'American Pillar' can be used as a ground cover. With a little prompting, it will grow vertically rather than horizontally and can be allowed to grow up an open-branched tree. If you don't mind a little effort training (see page 73), it can easily smother a pillar with bloom, or cover an archway or pergola.

## *Top Choice*

- 'Dr. W. Van Fleet' was introduced in 1910. This large and vigorous rambler measures 20 feet tall and 30 feet wide. It produces pointed buds that open to pale pink, fragrant flowers perched atop its long, slender stems.

## CLIMBERS VS. RAMBLERS

To the untrained eye, there doesn't seem to be a great deal of difference between a climbing rose and a so-called rambler. But indeed there are several:

- No doubt due to their more modern origins, climbers bloom repeatedly throughout summer (though some ramblers have been known to produce more blooms per plant, shorter bloom period notwithstanding).

- Climbers tend to have larger, more refined flowers, again thanks to the influence of modern breeding (some have a hybrid tea rose as a parent).

- Ramblers like to live up to their name—they grow rampantly. Climbers are perhaps a better choice for more formal settings.

## PRUNING RAMBLERS

True to their name, ramblers generate many canes unless you intervene. If your goal is to guide it up a support, limit it to four to eight canes, cutting away all others at the base. Do this in late winter or early spring while plants are still dormant.

# 'BLAZE'
## Climber

**Zones:** 5–9

**Size:** 8–12 ft. tall

**Bloom Time:** Mid-season, with excellent repeat

**Bloom Width:** 3 in.

**Fragrance:** Slight

**Thorniness:** Moderate

A first-rate performer, 'Blaze' produces plentiful clusters of cupped, semidouble, rich red flowers beginning in midsummer and repeating throughout the growing season. The blooms have a slight tea fragrance and up to twenty-four petals. Semiglossy, medium green foliage creates the perfect backdrop for its abundant red blooms. Remarkably healthy and vigorous, this large-flowered climber deserves its popularity. It is disease resistant and winter hardy.

### HOW TO GROW

Plant 'Blaze' in full sun in well-drained soil amended with lots of organic matter. Once it is established, cut out weak climbing shoots that are no longer productive. After bloom, prune the lateral, flowering shoots to the first set of five leaflets (about 3 inches long). Sometimes, however, you may want to train a vigorous lateral shoot to the framework to replace old, spent branches. 'Blaze' often gets black spot in summer. To control, apply fungicidal soap or sulfur in spring as leaves begin to emerge, and reapply as needed throughout the growing season. Handpick Japanese beetles if they are a problem.

## HOW TO USE

Because 'Blaze' grows quickly, has healthy and handsome foliage, and is a prolific bloomer, it makes an excellent choice for a trellis or a hedge. When planted as a climber, 'Blaze' makes a dramatic color impact in a small space. Plant several plants together to create a focal point in an expansive landscape. The flowers are splendid for bouquets.

## *Top Choices*

- 'Blaze Improved' is a selection of the original plant chosen for its large size and the abundance of its flowers. Today, most nurseries and catalogs are actually selling this 'Blaze' rather than the original.

- 'Paul's Scarlet Climber', probably a parent of 'Blaze', was introduced back in 1915 and won many awards in its day. It has similarly exuberant blooms, but it does not repeat much. It tends to grow a bit taller, to 15 feet.

## SUPPORT FOR CLIMBERS

Climbers, even thorny ones that grab at supports, need help to mount a support in an attractive manner and to stay attached. Appropriate supports include pillars, pergolas, a fence, a trellis—and even trees.

**1** Identify where you want your climber to grow and make sure that the support is sturdy and durable. A lush, flowering climber is heavy.

**2** After planting the climber, tie the canes to the support with soft, long-lasting material such as old panty hose or tights (the foliage will hide it from view in due course). To prevent chafing, try crossing the tie behind the cane so the tie is located between the cane and the support. Fan out the rose canes as much as possible.

**3** If your support is a fence or a trellis, resist the temptation to weave the canes in and out of the openings in the support. Eventually, this will make maintenance virtually impossible.

# 'CITY OF YORK'
## Climber

Zones: 5–9

Size: 15–20 ft. tall

Bloom Time: Mid-season, with no repeat

Bloom Width: 3–4 in.

Fragrance: Strong

Thorniness: Moderate

The abundant, creamy white blooms of 'City of York' have an open charm. Semidouble, saucer shaped, and very fragrant, they are not overfull with only fifteen petals each. They open to display a central tuft of frilly, bright gold stamens. 'City of York' has a long midseason bloom with no repeat. Winter hardy and disease resistant, it has glossy, medium green leaves. It grows tall, to 20 feet in some settings, with an upright, vigorous habit. Introduced in 1945, 'City of York' won the American Rose Society National Gold Medal Certificate in 1950.

### HOW TO GROW

'City of York' prefers a site in full sun with deep, well-drained soil amended with organic matter. After planting, do not prune for the first two growing seasons.

Prune established plants in late winter or early spring while they are still dormant. Remove one or two of the oldest canes and lightly cut back remaining stems. Sometimes, you may want to train a vigorous lateral shoot to the framework to replace old, spent branches.

### HOW TO USE

The lovely fragrance and form of 'City of York' enhance arches, pillars, pergolas, telephone poles, or walls. Since it has some shade tolerance, try growing it on an east wall around plants of a similarly soft hue to brighten the area and give it a bit of cottage-garden charm.

## *Top Choice*

• 'Sombreuil' is a shorter white climber, growing to about 10 feet tall. A climbing tea rose, it fares particularly well in the South (it's only hardy to Zone 7). Introduced in 1850, it has cupped, often quartered blooms with up to a hundred petals. It flowers in early to midseason with good repeat and is sweetly fragrant.

## CONTROLLING PESTS AND DISEASES

Controlling plant pests and diseases is not as overwhelming a task as it may seem. Many of the measures are preventative, day-to-day tasks that do not rely on pesticides. Observe plants each week for signs of trouble. That way you can treat a disease or infestation in the early stages when control is easiest.

Your normal gardening routine should include preventive measures. By cultivating soil regularly, you expose insect and disease-causing organisms to the sun and thus lessen their chances of survival. Spray plants with water to dislodge insects and remove dust. Pick off larger insects by hand. To discourage fungal leaf spots and blights, water plants in the morning and allow leaves to dry before nightfall. For the same reason, provide adequate air circulation around leaves and stems by giving plants sufficient space. Weeds provide a home for insects and diseases, so pull them up.

In fall, destroy infested and diseased canes, remove dead leaves and flowers, and clean up all plant debris. Do not add diseased or infested material to the compost pile.

# 'CLAIR MATIN'
## Climber

Zones: 5–9

Size: 10–12 ft. tall

Bloom Time: Mid-season, with reliable repeat

Bloom Width: 3 in.

Fragrance: Moderate

Thorniness: Moderate

The appeal of 'Clair Matin' lies in its lavish production of pink blooms and its reliable repeat. The scented flowers are a rather soft pink, of medium size, and sport twelve to eighteen petals. They're cupped to flat in shape and occur in clusters. Grown as a climber, 'Clair Matin' reaches a height of 10 to 12 feet. The habit is upright, rather arching, and vigorous, and the thorny canes carry glossy, dark green leaves. 'Clair Matin' won the Bagatelle Gold Medal in 1960.

### HOW TO GROW
'Clair Matin' prefers a sunny site in well-drained, rich soil generously amended with organic matter. Other than removing dead or damaged canes, do not prune for the first two growing seasons. Once established, prune in late winter or early spring when dormant. Remove

one or two of the oldest canes and prune the lateral, flowering shoots to the first set of five leaflets (about 3 inches long). 'Clair Matin' has some disease and pest resistance but benefits from scheduled spraying. Apply fungicidal soap or garden sulfur in spring as new leaves are emerging and repeat on a regular basis throughout the growing season. Watch for aphids and apply insecticidal soap to control.

### HOW TO USE

Trained as a climber, this lovely rose's prolific blooms bring warm color to walls, trellises, and archways. 'Clair Matin' also makes a nice freestanding shrub, with a potential height of 7 to 8 feet and a spread of about 5 feet. Try it in a mixed border, or plant several in a row to form a tall hedge.

## Top Choice

- 'Fashion', an award-winning floribunda rose, is a parent of 'Clair Matin' and worthy of consideration in its own right. An upright, bushy shrub, it grows to a height of 4 feet and has double, coral-pink blossoms with up to twenty-four petals borne singly and in clusters. Lightly scented, it blooms in midseason with excellent repeat.

## LET THE SUN SHINE

Growing a rose in full sun means that it needs at least 6 hours of sunshine a day. In selecting a site, remember that an area that receives morning sun is preferred over a site with afternoon sun; the goal is to have the dew dry quickly to prevent diseases.

It is easy to determine whether your roses are getting enough sun. Canes that are thin and spindly with few flowers and unusually large spaces between leaves are trying to tell you that their spot is too shaded. If this is the case, there are a number of steps you can take to help your plants:

❶ Move the plants to a sunnier site. This can be somewhat labor intensive, but it will solve the problem once and for all.

❷ If branches from nearby trees and hedges block the sun, try pruning them back. Pay attention to new growth and trim trees and shrubs regularly to keep the shadows from returning.

❸ Set up a reflecting screen behind roses. A simple one can be made by giving a sheet of plywood a coat of white paint.

# 'COMPASSION'
## Climber

Zones: 5–9

Size: 8–10 ft. tall

Bloom Time: All season

Bloom Width: 5 in.

Fragrance: Strong

Thorniness: Moderate

Luxuriant blossoms and an award-winning sweet fragrance draw gardeners to 'Compassion', a large-flowered climber that grows as tall as 10 feet. The double, salmon pink flowers shaded with apricot are showy and large, with thirty-six petals. They occur singly and in small clusters and bloom lavishly throughout the growing season. Disease resistant and winter hardy, 'Compassion' has an erect, bushy habit. The canes have dark green, semiglossy leaves and big red thorns.

### HOW TO GROW

'Compassion' grows best in full sun in well-drained soil to which lots of organic matter has been added. For the first three to four years, the only pruning required is the removal of dead and diseased canes in late winter or early spring. After that, you may remove the oldest canes as well to keep plants blooming vigorously. 'Compassion' has excellent disease resistance. Slugs sometimes damage the young leaves. To control, spread a layer of diatomaceous earth around the plant's root zone or install a strip of copper around each plant. (Copper strips are available from garden centers and catalogs.)

### HOW TO USE

'Compassion' is an excellent rose to grow up a pillar or pole. Because of its outstanding fragrance, site it where people can smell it, but not where its thorns would be a hazard. Keep it from encroaching onto paths or walkways so it doesn't snag people as they pass by. Try training it next to a porch or a window so you can enjoy its sweet scent indoors. It also makes a wonderful cut flower, thanks to its fragrance and elegant form. Grown unsupported, it makes a 7-foot-tall shrub; a row of this shrub makes a fine, tall hedge.

## Top Choices

- 'Highfield' is a pale yellow sport of 'Compassion', similar in all other respects.

- 'White Cockade', a parent of 'Compassion', is a short climber that bears beautifully shaped, pristine, double, white flowers set against large, dark green leaves. It can also be grown as a shrub and makes a lovely cut flower.

## BUYING ROSES

You can purchase roses from a nursery, in which case they often come in a container. Or you can order them from a mail-order catalog, in which case they are usually shipped bareroot. Container-grown roses are generally more expensive than bareroot plants and the selection is not as varied, however, they do have these noteworthy advantages:

- Buying a container-grown rose at a nursery allows you to see and touch the plant you are considering. You can judge for yourself if it looks healthy and strong.

- Container-grown roses can be transplanted into the garden for instant gratification, while bareroot roses take longer to establish themselves.

Before you buy a rose that you like, inspect it for flaws. The plant should have three to four shoots growing near the base. It should have a nice shape, without crossing branches. Also be sure to look for one that is not rootbound in its container; reject any with roots growing out the bottom holes.

# 'DON JUAN'
## Climber

Zones: 6–9

Size: 8–10 ft. tall

Bloom Time: Mid-season, with good repeat

Bloom Width: 5 in.

Fragrance: Strong

Thorniness: Moderate

Considered the best of the fragrant, dark red climbers, 'Don Juan' produces a profusion of large, 2-inch buds and velvety red, 5-inch flowers when it first comes into bloom in midseason. The double blooms, which have a potent rose scent, have thirty-five petals arranged in a classic, high-centered shape. The canes, 10 feet tall, are vigorous and erect, and the plant blooms on both old and new wood. 'Don Juan' has shiny, leathery, dark green foliage—a stunning background for the blooms. Flowers have the best color where nights are warm.

### HOW TO GROW

Plant 'Don Juan' in full sun in rich soil amended with organic matter. 'Don Juan' is not reliably winter hardy, however, it is disease resistant and does well in southern climates. In Zone 6, site the plants near a south-facing wall for added warmth and winter protection. Do not prune 'Don Juan' after planting or during the first three seasons' growth. Once it is established, cut out weak climbing shoots that are no longer productive. After blooming, prune the lateral, flowering shoots to the first set of five leaflets (about 3 inches long). After a few years, leave one vigorous lateral shoot to train the framework to replace old, spent branches. 'Don Juan' has moderate disease resistance and can show signs of black spot and mildew in late summer. To control, apply fungicidal soap in spring as leaves appear. Repeat as needed until frost. Aphids and rose midge can be controlled with applications of insecticidal soap; handpick Japanese beetles.

### HOW TO USE

'Don Juan' makes a handsome climber for pillars and trellises. It also makes an excellent hedge and looks good massed in the landscape. Because of its large flowers, heavy fragrance, and long, 16-inch stems, 'Don Juan' is ideal for bouquets.

## Top Choice

- 'Dublin Bay' is a more recent introduction (1975) and has large red blooms. It is hardier and perhaps more disease resistant than 'Don Juan', but it is also less fragrant.

## MILDEW CONTROL

Powdery mildew is spread by the wind and the spores germinate on young growth more often than on older leaves. Powdery mildew first appears as a raised blister and causes the affected leaf to crinkle and curl. It quickly develops into a white powder that spreads over leaves and flower buds, rendering the plant unsightly and eventually stunting growth.

Powdery mildew often appears when days are warm and nights are cool. It may also plague plantings that are overcrowded, so be sure to give your roses ample elbow room and to keep them well pruned for good air circulation. Thirsty plants also contract powdery mildew, so keep your roses well watered, especially during dry spells.

If despite your best efforts, early signs of the disease appear, immediately prune and dispose of the affected leaves or branches. Wash the leaves of your plants regularly with a stream of water from the hose. If necessary, spray a fungicide, making sure to follow the label directions exactly.

# 'DORTMUND'
## Climber

**Zones:** 4–9

**Size:** 10–12 ft. tall

**Bloom Time:** Mid-season, with good repeat

**Bloom Width:** 3 in.

**Fragrance:** Moderate

**Thorniness:** Very

Introduced in 1955, 'Dortmund' was hybridized by Kordes, the German rose breeder who created several extremely hardy roses. A tough and hardy climber, it produces large clusters of splendid, bright red flowers. They're single, consisting of five petals with a pure white eye and flashy gold stamens. The petals overlap, creating a ruffled contour, and the flower exudes an applelike perfume. Large hips appear after the flowers, but they should be removed early in the season to encourage further flowering. Later in the season, keep the hips for their handsome, orange-red autumn show. The leafy canes are equally attractive. Leaves are dark green and shiny, and thorns on the new growth tend to be flushed with red. Winter hardy and disease resistant, 'Dortmund' has an upright, vigorous habit.

## HOW TO GROW

'Dortmund' thrives in full sun and well-drained, organically rich soil. For the first three years after planting, prune out only dead or damaged wood in late winter. Thereafter, you can begin taking out older canes, again while the plant is dormant. 'Dortmund' has excellent disease resistance and is usually not troubled by pests. It is one of very few climbers that are reliably hardy in Zone 4.

## HOW TO USE

'Dortmund' makes a dramatic impact on pillars and trellises as a climber. Its bold colors show up well from a distance, so this is a good rose for training up a sunny wall at the far end of a yard or garden. Although its scent is pleasing and its looks are sensational, avoid planting 'Dortmund' where you might inadvertently brush against its thorny canes.

## Top Choice

- 'Leverkusen' is from the same breeder (introduced in 1954) and has creamy yellow, lightly scented flowers. It is a nice alternative if the red-and-white flowers of 'Dortmund' clash with a pastel color scheme. This climber reaches 10 feet tall.

# WATERING ROSES

Watering your roses deeply once a week will keep them far healthier than several quick watering sessions that just wet the surface of the soil. As a general rule, providing about 1 inch of water a week keeps roses healthy and nourished. It also promotes good root growth and drought tolerance, because roots are encouraged to delve deep. Some rules to water by:

**1** Avoid a strong blast from a hose, which may wash away mulch, expose fragile roots growing near the surface, and run off the surface rather than soaking the soil. Instead, water with the gentle spray from a watering wand or run the hose at a trickle.

**2** Never water your roses in the evening. Doing so encourages disease, because not much evaporation happens overnight.

**3** Don't splash water on the foliage or water from above. This creates standing pools of water that can lead to black spot and rust.

**4** If you prefer to hand-water your roses, try building a 3-inch wall of soil around the shrub's base so that you have what looks like a bowl made out of dirt. Fill it with water and allow this to soak into the soil. Repeat two times.

# 'NEW DAWN'

## Climber

Zones: 5–9

Size: 12–15 ft. tall, 8 ft. wide

Bloom Time: Mid-season, with good repeat

Bloom Width: 3 in.

Fragrance: Moderate

Thorniness: Moderate

Introduced in 1930, 'New Dawn' is a deservedly popular, large-flowered climber. It bears quantities of soft, shell pink flowers during the growing season; they have high centers when they first open, but as they age, the loosely double flowers open to reveal gold stamens. When fully open, the blossoms have thirty-five petals and emit a sweet rose fragrance. 'New Dawn' grows upright and rampant, reaching 15 feet tall and up to 8 feet wide. Disease resistant and winter hardy, it has moderately thorny canes and shiny, medium green leaves.

### How to Grow

'New Dawn' is a large-flowered climber that thrives in full sun in areas sheltered from winds. Set plants near a strong trellis or fence to give the vigorous canes adequate support. Amend the soil with organic matter and work it in well. For the first two to three years only, remove dead or damaged canes as needed. Afterward, you may improve the plant's profile and quality of bloom by taking out a couple of the older stems and trimming back the lateral stems. 'New Dawn' is not seriously troubled by pests or diseases, although slugs and aphids sometimes appear on the foliage. To control aphids, apply insecticidal soap; repeat as needed. Trap slugs by sinking margarine tubs into the ground and filling with beer.

## HOW TO USE

'New Dawn' has many uses. Because of its rampant growth, you can use it as a tall ground cover or train it on a wall, pillar, or sturdy trellis. It makes an excellent hedge or, massed in the landscape, a superb focal point. 'New Dawn' produces flowers suitable for cutting.

## Top Choice

- 'White Dawn', a descendant of 'New Dawn', produces clear white, semidouble blossoms about 3 inches wide with a sweet, gardenia-like fragrance. Measuring approximately 12 feet tall and 8 feet wide, it can be grown as a climber, a large shrub, a hedge, or massed in the landscape. It is winter hardy and disease resistant.

## GOOD SPORTS

The lovely climber 'New Dawn' originated as a "sport," or chance mutation, from a rambler called 'Dr. W. van Fleet'. Unlike its parent, it is generous with its repeat blooming. It also doesn't grow quite as tall (12 feet as opposed to 20 feet).

Other worthy roses have been known to generate climbing sports that have captured someone's attention and entered the nursery trade. 'Climbing Queen Elizabeth', 'Climbing Cecile Brunner', and 'Climbing Peace' are examples. However, some rosarians feel that such introductions are not always good roses—the climbing aspect is owed to lanky vegetative growth, often at the expense of flowering. So a good sport, especially a good climbing sport, is hard to find.

# 'BETTY PRIOR'
## Floribunda

**Zones:** 5–9

**Size:** 5–7 ft. tall,
2 ft. wide

**Bloom Time:** Mid-season, with reliable repeat

**Bloom Width:** 3 in.

**Fragrance:** Slight

**Thorniness:** Moderate

Profuse clusters of carmine pink, single blooms first appear on 'Betty Prior' in midseason. They look like dogwood flowers, with five petals that open cupped but become saucer shaped as they mature. They have a light, tea-rose fragrance. Initial bloom is heavy, with a lighter flower set for the rest of summer into early fall. 'Betty Prior' is a tall, upright bush with a rounded profile. Its canes are moderately thorny and covered with semiglossy, medium green leaves. Winter hardy and disease resistant, 'Betty Prior' thrives particularly in the North and tolerates a variety of growing conditions.

### HOW TO GROW

'Betty Prior' prefers a sunny site in well-drained soil that has some organic matter. To encourage the best floral display, cut back all stems by two-thirds while the plants are still dormant; fertilize with a complete rose fertilizer after pruning and again after the first flowers have faded. Deadhead spent flowers (see page 61). This rose is highly disease resistant and most years gets little or no black spot or powdery mildew. A spring application of fungicidal soap is good insurance against diseases in areas where weather conditions favor their development. Some insect pests, such as aphids and Japanese beetles, are occasional problems. Control aphids with insecticidal soap. Trap slugs by setting empty grapefruit halves upside down on the soil; check in the morning and discard if they contain slugs.

### HOW TO USE

'Betty Prior' creates a bright, showy effect when massed in the landscape. It also makes an excellent, long-blooming hedge. Its rounded shape and repeat bloom make it a good rose for a specimen planting, giving the effect of a pink dogwood in shrub form.

## Top Choices

- 'Kirsten Poulsen', a parent of 'Betty Prior', produces single, medium red blossoms on an upright bush that stands 4 feet tall. It makes a good specimen plant or hedge.

- 'Playgirl' is another single-flowered floribunda with clusters of stunning, hot pink blooms that show off bright gold stamens in their centers. It blooms a bit earlier with good repeat and is disease resistant.

## PRESSING ROSES

Single roses such as 'Betty Prior' are well suited to pressing. Use them in countless craft projects, including homemade greeting cards and for decorating candles and picture frames.

**1** Gather blooms on a dry, sunny day in midmorning, after the dew has dried.

**2** Scatter roses loosely on a piece of newspaper or blotter paper. Arrange them as you desire, but make sure the petals do not overlap.

**3** Place several pieces of paper between each layer of flowers.

**4** Put the stack in a warm, dry area and place heavy books or a board and bricks on top.

**5** After several weeks, gently peel back the layers of paper to see if the flowers have dried. If necessary, replace the paper with fresh paper to allow the roses to dry a bit longer.

# 'CLASS ACT'
## Floribunda

**Zones:** 5–9

**Size:** 3–4 ft. tall, 2–3 ft. wide

**Bloom Time:** Mid-season, with reliable repeat

**Bloom Width:** 3 in.

**Fragrance:** Slight

**Thorniness:** Moderate

'Class Act' is just that—an elegant white bloomer that was chosen for both an All-America Rose Selection Award and a Portland Gold Medal in 1989. Pure white, semidouble blooms with twenty petals and a slight, fruity scent appear in midseason and repeat well throughout summer. The petals are loosely arranged in flat blossoms that occur in clusters of three to six. The bushy plant is covered with dark green, semiglossy leaves and the canes have long, narrow thorns. This rose is disease resistant and winter hardy.

### HOW TO GROW

Plant 'Class Act' in a sunny location in well-drained soil generously amended with organic matter. Prune to encourage heavy flowering by cutting back the stems by one-half to two-thirds each winter or early spring. Like other white-flowered roses, it looks best if the spent flowers are removed throughout the season. 'Class Act' has excellent disease resistance but is sometimes troubled by insects such as aphids. To control, apply insecticidal soap.

## HOW TO USE

Thanks to its compact size and repeat bloom, 'Class Act' looks terrific in a mixed border with perennials. It makes a lovely low hedge that is long blooming. It also creates a charming effect when massed in groups of at least three. For a simple but stunning island bed, surround three or five 'Class Act' roses with a row of matching maroon-and-pink coleus, or a single color of dark-leaved New Guinea impatiens.

## *Top Choices*

- 'French Lace' has a similar profile but the flowers are creamier, almost a porcelain pink. They're also a bit more fragrant. Also bred by Bill Warriner, it was released in 1980 and won an All-America Rose Selection Award in 1982.

- 'Regensberg' has white at the base of each petal and on the reverse, but the tops look as though they have been brushed with rosy pink paint. Only 1½ to 2 feet tall, this rose blends well with most perennials.

## LOCATION, LOCATION

When siting your roses, remember that most need 6 to 8 hours of sunlight a day. If possible, plant your roses with a southern exposure so the morning sun can dry the dew and help prevent fungal diseases from taking hold. Late-afternoon shade helps blooms maintain their color and protects bushes from the peak heat of the day.

Most roses benefit from wind protection and good air circulation. Ever-blooming roses such as hybrid teas are particularly heavy feeders. Grow them where they can avoid competing with other hungry plants for the necessary nutrients.

## WHAT IS A FLORIBUNDA?

In the fifty or so years since floribundas were first developed, the definition has changed. Most rosarians agree that "floribunda" means a shrubby rose that carries its well-formed blooms in clusters instead of one to a stem. They are usually more refined than some old-fashioned shrub roses, growing to less than 4 feet tall and maintaining a fairly compact habit.

# 'EUROPEANA'
## Floribunda

**Zones:** 5–9

**Size:** 2½–3 ft. tall, 2 ft. wide

**Bloom Time:** Mid-season, with good repeat

**Bloom Width:** 3 in.

**Fragrance:** Slight

**Thorniness:** Moderate

This vigorous and bushy plant produces deep crimson, show-quality blooms. The flowers are cupped and semidouble with fifteen to twenty petals and a light tea fragrance. They bloom profusely in big clusters in midseason and repeat reliably thereafter. 'Europeana' has a rounded habit with bronze to reddish new foliage that ages to dark green. Its canes are moderately thorny. It performs best in areas with hot summers. Considered the best of all red floribundas, 'Europeana' was an All-America Rose Selection in 1968.

### HOW TO GROW

'Europeana' prefers locations with full sun but grows and flowers well in spots that receive 1 or 2 hours of light shade. Set plants in well-drained soil to which organic matter has been added. To promote heavy flowering, prune while dormant, cutting back the stems by two-thirds. 'Europeana' requires winter protection in Zone 5. It has some resistance to diseases but shows signs of black spot in summer and early fall. To control, apply fungicidal soap in spring when leaves begin to emerge; repeat as needed throughout summer. If insects such as aphids appear, apply insecticidal soap as needed.

### HOW TO USE

'Europeana' makes a wonderful bedding rose. To draw attention to its blooms, surround it with annuals and perennials (or other short roses) that bloom in pastel shades of yellow, cream, or peach. Foliage plants with silver leaves also act as a good foil. Planted en masse or as a hedge, the contrast between its dark red flowers and dark green leaves creates garden drama.

## Top Choices

- 'Showbiz', an All-America Rose Selection in 1985, is another, similar floribunda with medium red flowers set against dark green leaves. Its petals are more ruffled than those of 'Europeana', and the flowers are fuller, with up to thirty petals.

- 'Trumpeter', named for Louis Armstrong, is similar to 'Europeana' but with a warmer, more orange-red color, more petals (thirty-five to forty-five), and a lighter scent.

## THE LOWDOWN ON BLACK SPOT

This common rose disease is caused by a fungus and appears as small, round black spots on the leaves, usually during rainy or humid weather. As the disease progresses, the fringed spots enlarge and gain a yellow halo. Eventually, the leaves turn entirely yellow and fall off.

To prevent black spot from occurring, water your rosebushes at ground level. Make sure they get good air circulation, which may mean thinning them or taking out or cutting back nearby plants. Rake up and dispose of any fallen leaves. Spray in late spring with a fungicide listed as controlling black spot and continue all season.

If your plants become afflicted:

- Remove all affected leaves and canes and dispose of them; they will never recover. Leave healthy ones alone.

- Spray with sulfur, use either a dormant spray of lime sulfur or sulfur dust. (Note that these products are toxic; take proper precautions and follow label directions carefully.)

- Spray leaves with a baking-soda solution—5 tablespoons baking soda to 5 gallons water, with several drops of dish detergent added to help it stick. (This spray is also good for powdery mildew.)

# 'ICEBERG'
## Floribunda

Zones: 5–9

Size: 4 ft. tall

Bloom Time: Early to midseason, with all-season repeat

Bloom Width: 3 in.

Fragrance: Moderate

Thorniness: Moderate

Renowned for the beauty of its pristine white flowers, 'Iceberg' starts blooming in early to midseason and continues all season long. It is floriferous, producing abundant clusters of fragrant flowers with thirty petals. The hybrid-tea-shaped flowers open to a cupped shape, revealing a central tuft of showy gold stamens. This tough, hardy floribunda is also extremely disease resistant, except to black spot, and vigorous. It has upright, bushy growth and light green, semiglossy leaves. 'Iceberg' won a Royal National Rose Society Gold Medal in 1958.

### HOW TO GROW
'Iceberg' thrives in a sunny location in soil that is fertile and well drained. For best flower production, prune plants when dormant, cutting canes back by two-thirds.

Fertilize with a complete rose fertilizer after pruning and again after the first flowers have faded. Deadhead spent flowers to encourage continual bloom. This beautiful rose is vulnerable to diseases such as black spot and powdery mildew, so give it extra protection to keep it looking its best. Aphids and Japanese beetles can become bothersome in summer. To control, apply an insecticidal soap as needed.

### HOW TO USE

'Iceberg' makes an impressive hedge and is well suited to mass plantings.

## Top Choices

- 'Ivory Fashion', an All-America Rose Selection for 1959, is worth considering if your color scheme calls for a creamy white. The semidouble, 3-inch flowers have fifteen to eighteen petals and an open form with yellow stamens. The bush is vigorous and upright, growing 3 to 4 feet tall.

- 'Saratoga', a winner in 1964, has large, 4-inch flowers, a similar petal count (thirty to thirty-five), and a powerful fragrance.

### WINTER MULCH

When the cold starts to descend in late fall and early winter, roses begin to go dormant. Even if you expect good snow cover, your roses will appreciate additional protection to help them through the winter months.

**1** Take soil from elsewhere in your yard and make a 1-foot mound all around the base of the plant.

**2** On top of the soil, add a layer of mulch. To the sides of the mound add leaves, pine needles, or wood chips.

**3** Do not prepare the plant for winter too early. The added insulation will cause the plant's temperature to warm and could cause late-season growth that will delay dormancy.

# 'MARGARET MERRIL'
## Floribunda

**Zones:** 5–9

**Size:** 4 ft. tall, 3 ft. wide

**Bloom Time:** Early to midseason, with good repeat

**Bloom Width:** 4 in.

**Fragrance:** Strong

**Thorniness:** Moderate

One of the most fragrant floribundas, 'Margaret Merril' combines perfect, hybrid-tea-shaped blossoms with a potent perfume redolent of citrus and spice. The result is an internationally acclaimed rose with buff-colored buds opening into large, ruffled, satin white blooms flushed with palest pink. Flowers have twenty-eight petals, bloom all season, and may grow even larger in moderate temperatures. They appear on an upright, well-branched, vigorous bush. Moderately thorny canes are covered with large, somewhat shiny, medium green leaves.

### HOW TO GROW
'Margaret Merril' is easy to grow. It prefers at least 6 hours of sun per day but will tolerate some shade. It flowers best in moist, fertile soil with good drainage.

Prune it annually in late winter or early spring, taking out dead or damaged canes and reducing others by about one-third. As with most white-flowered roses, the fading petals discolor quickly so deadhead them promptly (see page 61). You'll be rewarded with additional blooms.

### HOW TO USE

'Margaret Merril' looks nice in massed plantings (three or more) grouped together or planted with other roses, especially those in shades of pink. You may also use it as a low-growing shrub. Be sure to locate it near a garden bench, path, or entryway so you can appreciate the delicious fragrance. It blends well with any other color.

## Top Choices

- 'Pascali', the striking hybrid tea rose, is one parent of 'Margaret Merril'. An All-America Rose Selection for 1969 and winner of numerous international awards, 'Pascali' has creamy white, double flowers (thirty petals) 4 inches wide, with a classic, hybrid tea form. It blooms abundantly all season on fairly thorny canes. Disease resistant and winter hardy, it stands 3 to 4 feet tall.

- 'First Kiss' is a similar plant but with a more pronounced pink flower color. It has plenty of semiglossy green foliage for contrast.

### ROSES IN YOUR CHRISTMAS TREE

Dainty dried rose blossoms, plump buds, even leaves can be a surprising and elegant addition to a Christmas tree. Whether they are attached to ornaments or distributed among the limbs, these souvenirs of the past summer add a festive dash of resplendent color. Fastening them to ornaments is easy; just use a hot glue gun. Then spray with a clear sealer (available from a hobby store) to secure the dried materials and to prevent them from absorbing moisture.

### WHO WAS MARGARET MERRIL?

This enchanting rose was named by Jack Harkness, the English nurseryman who introduced it in 1978, for the fictitious spokeswoman for the popular face cream Oil of Olay. Since then, several real Margaret Merrils have come forward, who reportedly enjoy growing the bush in their own gardens.

# 'MISTER LINCOLN'
## Hybrid Tea

**Zones:** 5–9

**Size:** 4–5 ft. tall, 2–3 ft. wide

**Bloom Time:** All season

**Bloom Width:** 5 in.

**Fragrance:** Strong

**Thorniness:** Moderate

'Mister Lincoln' produces large flowers of dark velvety red that start as pointed buds. As the flowers mature, they exhibit a classic, high-centered shape and then develop a cupped form filled with thirty to forty petals. They exude a vibrant damask-rose scent. Set against rich, leathery, dark green leaves, the flowers dazzle with their outstanding beauty and powerful scent. An All-America Rose Selection for 1965, 'Mister Lincoln' has an upright, well-branched form. It is disease resistant and winter hardy.

### HOW TO GROW

One of the more beautiful hybrid tea roses, 'Mister Lincoln' needs extra attention to stay healthy and look its best. Plant in an open, lightly breezy area in full sun. Amend the soil with lots of organic matter. Prune when dormant, cutting back all canes by two-thirds and removing any thin or diseased stems. Fertilize in spring after pruning and again when the first blossoms fade. Apply a fungicidal soap or garden sulfur in spring and repeat applications as needed throughout the growing season. If pests such as aphids appear, treat with insecticidal soap.

### HOW TO USE

Use 'Mister Lincoln' in massed plantings or as a hedge. The bush's form is a bit stiff for any but the most formal flower gardens; it looks better in the company of other hybrid tea roses. Because of its long stems and glorious blooms, it makes an excellent cut flower. Plant enough so you can cut several blooms without ruining the display.

## Top Choices

- 'Chrysler Imperial', one parent of 'Mister Lincoln', has won numerous awards for looks and fragrance and was an All-America Rose Selection for 1953. Its deep red, damask-scented flowers are double, with forty to fifty petals and a classic, high-centered shape that opens to a well-balanced, shapely bloom. 'Chrysler Imperial' grows best in hot climates. Grown in cool, wet conditions, this 4- to 5-foot-tall bush can develop mildew on its dark green leaves.

- 'Ingrid Bergman', a favorite in Europe, has superb, rich red flowers; unfortunately, they are scentless. The plant is quite disease resistant.

## HOMEMADE ROSE OIL

A popular addition to bathwater, rose oil is easy to make. Use two to six drops per bath, adjusting to your preference.

**1** Fill a medium-sized glass jar with rose petals. Do not pack the petals too firmly.

**2** Fill the jar with sunflower oil and secure the cap.

**3** Place the jar in a warm, dark place such as an attic or basement.

**4** After a day or two, strain the oil into a large bowl. Clean the jar, fill with new rose petals, and fill with the strained oil. Fix the cap tightly and let sit. Repeat in ten to fourteen days.

**5** After that, occasionally check the fragrance of the oil. When it attains the desired intensity, strain once again and refrigerate. It will last up to a year.

# 'NEARLY WILD'
## Floribunda

**Zones:** 5–9

**Size:** 3–4 ft. tall

**Bloom Time:** All season

**Bloom Width:** 2–3 in.

**Fragrance:** Slight

**Thorniness:** Moderate

The radiant rose-pink flowers on 'Nearly Wild' add mounds of spectacularly bright color to the landscape. The flowers, which have a light apple scent, are single, with just five petals, and are carried in clusters. Floriferous and hardy, 'Nearly Wild' blooms throughout the season, unlike the wild roses it resembles. This compact, rounded bush does best in cool climates and slightly acidic soil.

### HOW TO GROW

'Nearly Wild' prefers at least 6 hours of sun per day. It flowers best in fertile soil with good drainage. Prune the plants when dormant, cutting back all canes by one-half and removing dead and diseased ones. 'Nearly Wild' is susceptible to black spot and powdery mildew if you crowd it too close to other plants. To keep it healthy, this particular rose needs excellent air circulation. Apply fungicidal soap in spring as leaves are emerging and again as needed to control diseases.

## HOW TO USE

For maximum show, plant 'Nearly Wild' massed in the landscape, or as a hedge. As you might gather from the name, its relaxed form makes good transition to less manicured portions of the yard. Its never-ending blooms and compact stature earn it a place in any informal planting, including a casual foundation planting or mixed border.

## Top Choices

- 'Pink Meidiland' is a shrub rose with slightly smaller blooms. It produces eye-catching single flowers with five deep pink petals and a white center. They have no scent, unfortunately, but bloom prolifically in midseason, with a second flush in fall.

- 'Dainty Bess' is a hybrid tea rose, but you'd never guess that from its flat, single flowers and rugged nature. The blooms are medium to light pink with unusual dark reddish stamens in their centers. Fragrance is an added bonus.

## "HEELING IN" A ROSE

If you buy a bareroot rose but are unable to plant it right away, or if a rose nursery happens to ship you one a bit early, you will need to heel it in. A bareroot rose can remain in such a setting for a week or more, provided you take good care of it—in particular, don't let it dry out.

❶ Dig a sloping trench in a spot that is shaded. Make it about a foot deep and at a 45-degree angle to the surface of the garden bed. Keep the removed soil nearby, because you will soon need it.

❷ Place the rosebush in the sloping trench, positioning the roots at the bottom.

❸ Use the soil to fill in the trench around the roots and stem of the rose. Water well to settle the soil. Be sure to keep the soil moist.

# 'PEACE'
## Hybrid Tea

**Zones:** 5–9

**Size:** 5–6 ft. tall, 2½ ft. wide

**Bloom Time:** All season

**Bloom Width:** 6 in.

**Fragrance:** Slight to none

**Thorniness:** Moderate

Possibly the most widely known of all roses, 'Peace' produces large yellow flowers edged in pink. The big blooms are double, with forty to forty-five petals and a faint, fruity scent. The flowers exhibit a classic, high-centered, hybrid tea shape. When fully open, the blossom may reveal a divided center, but overall its mature shape is large, full, and pleasing. Disease resistant and winter hardy, 'Peace' has large, shiny, dark green foliage and somewhat thorny canes. It has won awards throughout North America and Europe, including a designation as an All-America Rose Selection in 1946.

### HOW TO GROW

'Peace' prefers at least 6 hours of sun per day but can tolerate a bit of shade. It flowers best in moist, ordinary to fertile soil with good drainage and grows best east of the Rocky Mountains. Prune in late winter or early spring when plants are dormant; remove any dead and diseased canes and lightly cut back remaining stems. Fertilize with a complete rose fertilizer after pruning. To control black spot and mildew, spray the young leaves with fungicidal soap, repeating every few weeks throughout the growing season. Control insects by applying insecticidal soap as needed. In Zone 5, plants need winter protection to prevent damage (see page 93).

### HOW TO USE

Use 'Peace' as a specimen, since on its own it can make an impressive sight. Although most hybrid teas look better when planted close together because of their upright, narrow, or sometimes scraggly habits, 'Peace' is a full enough shrub to be planted on its own. Its blooms make excellent cut flowers.

## Top Choices

- 'Chicago Peace' is a sport of the original; the main difference is that its flowers are deeper pink, with more ruffled petals. They may also be more fragrant.

- 'Climbing Peace' grows 12 feet tall and is suitable for training on a trellis or wall. This fragrant yellow rose edged in pink may take several years to establish itself. Until that time, its blooms may be scarce. Zones 6 to 9.

## PREVENTING DISEASE

A fungal disease or virus can ruin a year of hard work and planning in the garden. However, diseases can be prevented in large part by taking a few precautions:

**1** Be careful with water. A garden that is perpetually damp provides a good place for black spot to germinate. Conversely, a plant that is kept too dry will be susceptible to powdery mildew.

**2** Remove dead leaves, spent flowers, and prunings from your garden; don't let them collect at the base of the bushes. Black spot spores are often found on fallen leaves.

**3** Careful pruning allows for good air circulation around each plant. This in turn will help the leaves dry and will reduce the likelihood of fungal infection.

**4** When fertilizing, follow label directions. Overfertilizing causes lush leaf growth that invites disease.

# 'QUEEN ELIZABETH'
## Grandiflora

Zones: 5–9

Size: 5–7 ft. tall,
2½–3 ft. wide

Bloom Time: Mid-
season, with excellent
repeat

Bloom Width: 4 in.

Fragrance: Moderate

Thorniness: Moderate

The first, best, and by far most popular grandiflora, 'Queen Elizabeth' produces substantial pink flowers with up to forty petals each. The large, double, pink blossoms have a high-centered to cupped form and a moderate tea fragrance, and they bloom constantly. They appear singly and in small, long-stemmed clusters. Disease-resistant 'Queen Elizabeth' has shiny, leathery, dark green leaves and somewhat thorny canes. It has won awards throughout North America and Europe, including a designation as an All-America Rose Selection in 1955.

### HOW TO GROW
Plant 'Queen Elizabeth' in a location with full sun in well-drained soil that has been amended with plenty of organic matter. In late winter or early spring while

plants are dormant, remove dead and damaged canes. Cut back remaining stems by one-half to three-quarters to promote the best flowering and vigorous growth. Fertilize with a balanced rose fertilizer after pruning and again after the first flowers fade. Remove spent blooms to encourage the production of more flowers and reduce the spread of diseases. In Zone 5, mound loose soil around the graft in fall after the ground has frozen (see page 93). 'Queen Elizabeth' often shows signs of black spot and mildew in summer. To control, apply a fungicidal soap in early spring and repeat as needed. Control insects such as aphids with insecticidal soap.

### HOW TO USE

With its long stems and large, beautiful blossoms, 'Queen Elizabeth' makes a fabulous cut flower. Because of its tall stature, you can plant it behind shorter shrubs or roses for a fuller look, or use it on its own in hedges or bold massed plantings.

## Top Choices

- 'Queen Elizabeth, Climbing' is a sport that grows 14 feet tall and is suitable for training up a fence or wall. Flowering on old wood, it produces prolific numbers of grand pink flowers once it's established.

- 'White Lightnin', a 1980 introduction, has fragrant white blooms in clusters on long stems; the plant is much shorter than 'Queen Elizabeth' but is still considered a grandiflora. It reaches 4 to 5 feet tall.

## FERTILIZING ROSES

Roses are greedy eaters but reward you with strong growth and plenty of flowers. Use a balanced or rose fertilizer and follow label directions for the correct amount.

**1** At planting time, add slow-release fertilizer to the planting hole. Also feed when you prune each spring.

**2** Beginning right after the first flush of blooms fades, feed new and established roses monthly during the growing season, stopping six to eight weeks before frost.

**3** Sprinkle fertilizer evenly around the plant at the "drip line" (the imaginary circle around the outer edge of the leaves). Scratch it in with a trowel or cultivator and water well.

### 'QUEEN ELIZABETH' THE FIRST

Grandiflora is a small and fairly new rose class, the first of its kind being 'Queen Elizabeth' in 1954. Grandifloras supposedly combine the elegant flowers and long stems of hybrid tea roses with the floribundas' bloom clusters and hardiness. Although they are taller and more vigorous than floribundas and hybrid teas, they will not tolerate cold winters.

# 'SUNSPRITE'
## Floribunda

**Zones:** 5–9

**Size:** 2–3 ft. tall, 2–3 ft. wide

**Bloom Time:** Mid-season, with good repeat

**Bloom Width:** 3 in.

**Fragrance:** Strong

**Thorniness:** Moderate

The blooms of 'Sunsprite' create a golden glow in the landscape. The deep yellow, double flowers have a full, cupped form (with twenty-eight petals) and occur in clusters on a compact shrub. When the buttery blooms open wide, they look somewhat ruffled and frilly, with deep orange-gold stamens. Although they are striking in color, it is their scent—a sweet, powerful, licorice perfume—that you will remember. Winter hardy and disease resistant, 'Sunsprite' prefers cooler temperatures. It has a bushy, robust, erect habit and moderately thorny canes covered with shiny, deep green leaves.

### HOW TO GROW

Plant 'Sunsprite' in a bright sunny location in soil that has been generously amended with organic matter. Prune when plants are dormant, cutting back all canes by two-thirds. Deadhead spent flowers to encourage continuous bloom. 'Sunsprite' has good resistance to black spot and powdery mildew, but in certain weather conditions these diseases can be troublesome. Control with garden sulfur or fungicidal soap applied to the new leaves as they emerge in spring; reapply as needed throughout the growing season. If insects appear, treat plants with an application of insecticidal soap and repeat as needed.

### HOW TO USE

For the maximum show, plant 'Sunsprite' massed in the landscape. You can also plant it in a bed of roses or facing down a taller shrub. To draw attention to this rose, surround it with flowers in any pastel hue. For a bolder effect, include some companions of brighter or darker hues such as blue lobelias or 'Ruby Veil' coralbells.

## Top Choice

• 'Sun Flare', another yellow floribunda ('Sunsprite' is a parent), has quality lemon yellow blooms, also a licorice fragrance, and is hardy to Zone 5 with winter protection.

## SAVVY SPACING

When installing a rose bed or a hedge of roses, adequate spacing is important, not just for the appearance but also for sufficient air circulation. Crowded plants are more susceptible to disease. Planting distance depends on several factors, including the length of the growing season and the kinds of roses you grow.

With a longer growing season, rosebushes planted in the South tend to grow larger. Therefore, you would plant hybrid tea or grandiflora roses at least 3 feet apart—on all sides—in the South. In the mid-Atlantic or central states, space them at least 2 feet. About 18 inches apart is sufficient in the northernmost states.

Plant smaller floribunda roses closer together—30 inches apart in warm climates and 18 inches apart in cold climates. Vigorous old garden roses, on the other hand, need more space to grow. Depending on their habits, they may require as much as 10 feet between plants.

# 'TOUCH OF CLASS'
## Hybrid Tea

**Zones:** 5–9

**Size:** 4–5 ft. tall, 3 ft. wide

**Bloom Time:** All season

**Bloom Width:** 5 in.

**Fragrance:** Slight to none

**Thorniness:** Moderate

A popular exhibition rose, 'Touch of Class' produces large coral-pink blooms shaded orange and cream with a perfect, high-centered, hybrid tea form. The large blooms are double, with thirty-three petals and a soft tea fragrance. Disease resistant and winter hardy, 'Touch of Class' has shiny, dark green foliage and somewhat thorny canes. New growth is a mahogany, enhancing the richness of the coral-pink blooms, which keep their pinpoint centers as the buds unfurl. 'Touch of Class' has an erect, bushy habit. It was an All-America Rose Selection in 1984.

### HOW TO GROW

'Touch of Class' does best in a sunny, lightly breezy location in soil that is well drained and amended with lots of organic matter. Prune in spring when plants are dormant, cutting back all canes by two-thirds and removing any thin stems. Deadhead spent flowers to encourage heavy bloom. Fertilize with a balanced fertilizer (see page 103). To control diseases, particularly mildew, apply garden sulfur or fungicidal soap in spring and repeat as needed throughout the season. If insects such as aphids become a problem, apply an insecticidal soap.

### HOW TO USE

The long stems on 'Touch of Class', its uniquely colorful petals, and its perfect form make it an ideal cut flower. Grow it in a rose bed with other hybrid teas and floribundas, where it will be an impressive sight.

## Top Choices

- 'Touch of Class' is also available as a climbing rose.

- 'Sheer Elegance', released a few years later and also an All-America Rose Selection (in 1991), also winningly combines shades of coral, pink, and orange. The color is deeper at the petal edges, the blooms are a little larger (5 to 6 inches wide), and they have a slight scent. Like those of 'Touch of Class', they are of exhibition quality.

## THE FINEST ROSES?

Hybrid tea roses are the most popular and widely grown roses worldwide, probably for their bloom quality more than anything else. A large, elegantly formed, high-centered, often fragrant blossom, one to a long cutting stem, is exactly what many people want in a rose. Plus, hybrid teas produce these beauties continuously through summer, a claim some other beloved roses cannot match.

Older hybrid teas were bred mainly for the florist trade and the plants were not particularly handsome, bushy, fragrant, or disease resistant. Modern-day rose breeding has improved and refined them, however. You can now expect a handsome, upright-growing bush laden with foliage.

The flaws of lanky habit and susceptibility to pests and diseases continue to be a challenge to hybrid tea breeders—but many gardeners are willing to trim, spray, and otherwise pamper the bushes just to get a bounty of the fabulous flowers.

# 'TROPICANA'
## Hybrid Tea

Zones: 5–9

Size: 4–5 ft. tall, 3 ft. wide

Bloom Time: All season

Bloom Width: 5 in.

Fragrance: Moderate

Thorniness: Moderate to very

Vivid orange color and classic form make 'Tropicana' a superstar among roses. Actually, this rose is known as 'Super Star' in Europe, where it was introduced in 1960. It produces large blooms with thirty to thirty-five petals and a classic, high-centered, hybrid tea form. The blossoms have a sweet, fruity scent and bloom plentifully. 'Tropicana' has large pointed buds and fairly shiny, dark green foliage on long, rather thorny stems. It has an erect, well-branched, bushy habit. It was an All-America Rose Selection in 1963.

### HOW TO GROW
'Tropicana' prefers at least 6 hours of sun per day but will tolerate a little shade. It flowers best in moist, fertile soil with good drainage. Prune in spring before new growth begins, cutting back all canes by two-thirds and

removing any thin, spindly growth. To control black spot, powdery mildew, and other diseases, apply a fungicidal soap or garden sulfur to new leaves in spring and repeat monthly throughout the growing season. If pests such as aphids appear, apply an insecticidal soap as needed. 'Tropicana' is more prone to mildew when grown in dry regions of the western states.

### HOW TO USE

'Tropicana' looks striking massed in a rose bed. It is an attractive cut flower; you may wish to grow an extra bush in an out-of-the-way location so you can cut often for arrangements without diminishing the display.

## Top Choices

- 'Tropicana, Climbing' is also available as a climber, though you'll have to do a little searching to track it down.

- 'Fragrant Cloud' is another brightly colored, big-flowered hybrid tea. It is a rich coral-red and, as you might guess from the name, has a wonderfully strong true-rose fragrance.

- 'Brandy' offers a lighter shade of rich orange, almost apricot. Also a hybrid tea, its flowers are large and fragrant.

## GETTING READY FOR WINTER

In areas with cold winters, hybrid teas need winter protection:

**1** Cease fertilizer applications six weeks before the first frost to discourage late-season growth.

**2** Stop deadheading faded blooms in fall to retard the plant's growth.

**3** Water your roses thoroughly before the ground freezes.

**4** Tie the canes together; remove any remaining leaves from the plant and from the rose bed to prevent disease.

**5** Make a chicken-wire cage around the rose. Pile a foot of soil over the base of the plant, then fill the cage with a foot of compost, salt hay, leaves, or other mulch. Or use mounded dirt and a top mulch without a cage. Do not bare the rose until the danger of frost is past in spring.

# 'CINDERELLA'
## Miniature

**Zones:** 4–9 with protection, 6–9 without protection

**Size:** 8–10 in. tall, 10 in. wide

**Bloom Time:** Midseason, with excellent repeat

**Bloom Width:** 1 in.

**Fragrance:** Strong

**Thorniness:** Moderate

'Cinderella' is small even for a miniature and so is sometimes called a "micro-mini" rose. It produces tiny, pale pink to white flowers in abundance. The double blossoms are cup shaped, with forty-five petals packed tightly in even rows. An intense, spicy fragrance adds to the appeal of these blooms, which appear singly and in clusters. 'Cinderella' blooms profusely in midseason with excellent repeat. Disease resistant and winter hardy, the little bush has a compact, erect habit and rather shiny, medium green leaves. Though one of the earlier cultivars in this class, it remains one of the most popular.

### HOW TO GROW
Plant 'Cinderella' in a sunny location that is sheltered from strong winds. Plant in well-drained, organically

rich soil. Prune in spring as buds begin to grow, cutting back canes to two or three buds. Deadhead spent flowers to encourage increased flowering. Fertilize after pruning in spring and again after the first round of flowering. 'Cinderella' is rarely troubled by pests or diseases.

### HOW TO USE

'Cinderella' is charming when it is massed in beds of miniature roses used to edge beds of full-sized roses, or planted to create a short hedge. Groups of three of more work nicely in perennial borders. You can also grow it in a container; it's a good choice for the limited space of a (sunny) urban courtyard. It makes a wonderful cut flower to bring indoors. In warm climates with plenty of light, try 'Cinderella' indoors as a houseplant, in a greenhouse, or under grow lights.

## *Top Choices*

- 'Cinderella Gold' is a similar compact and thornless micro-mini rose, but with yellow buds and double blossoms.

- 'Small Miracle' is a traditionally sized miniature (18 inches tall) that produces 2-inch ivory blossoms.

## GROWING MINIS INDOORS

Just as they do outdoors, potted indoor miniature roses adore sunshine, so place them on a windowsill in a room that faces south; they should get at least 6 hours a day.

If that's not possible, or to provide supplementary light, place them under fluorescent lights for up to 16 hours a day, using a timer if necessary. Place them within a few inches of the light. The more light they get, the more flowers they'll produce.

Of course, you must also keep the soil mix moist and fertilize regularly during the growing season as you would for any rose.

# 'JEAN KENNEALLY'
## Miniature

**Zones:** 4–9 with adequate winter protection, 6–9 unprotected

**Size:** 22–30 in. tall, 12 in. wide

**Bloom Time:** Midseason, with excellent repeat

**Bloom Width:** 2 in.

**Fragrance:** Slight

**Thorniness:** Moderate

Luscious apricot color and a classic hybrid tea form characterize the elegant blooms of 'Jean Kenneally'. The blossoms are lightly fragrant and double, with twenty-four to thirty petals. This lovely miniature rose flowers in midseason and has abundant repeat blooms. Upright, vigorous, and bushy, 'Jean Kenneally' stands over 2 feet, fairly tall for a miniature. It is disease resistant and winter hardy, with somewhat glossy, medium green leaves. 'Jean Kenneally' won the American Rose Society Award of Excellence in 1986.

### HOW TO GROW

'Jean Kenneally' thrives in full sun in rich, well-drained soil amended with generous amounts of organic matter. Prune in late winter or early spring when the plant is dormant. Remove any dead or diseased stems, then cut the remaining canes back by one-half. 'Jean Kenneally' is sometimes troubled by black spot late in the season. Control with a fungicidal soap and try to keep the foliage as dry as possible. Control spider mites with an insecticidal soap.

### HOW TO USE
Because of the upright, bushy stature of 'Jean Kenneally', it is an excellent rose for a massed bed. Its apricot blossoms, size, and long season of bloom make it a welcome addition to any flower border, formal or informal. 'Jean Kenneally' can also be grown in a container or cultivated indoors. It makes a nice cut flower and has proved to be a popular exhibition rose.

## Top Choices

- 'Heavenly Days' is similar, growing to between 15 and 20 inches high; the flowers have more yellow in them. It won an American Rose Society Award of Excellence in 1988.

- 'Loving Touch' is an apricot-flowered miniature with compact growth. It is another recipient of the American Rose Society Award of Excellence. Growing up to 18 inches tall with a rounded habit, 'Loving Touch' produces double blooms with twenty to twenty-five petals and a light tea fragrance.

## FIGHTING SPIDER MITES

Miniature roses, especially, seem to be vulnerable to spider mites. These are tiny red or brown insects that dwell on leaf bottoms. They are adept at scraping plant tissue and feeding off the juices that well up in the scarred area.

**1** Diagnose the problem. Signs that spider mites are attacking include: lower leaves of the bush turn yellow, pale, and/or dry; plant growth is stunted; very fine webs appear on leaves.

**2** Spray the undersides of the leaves to wash them off. Take care not to use too much water pressure or you could damage the stems.

**3** Repeat the procedure each time you water. Any insects that try to return to the cleaned plant will be whisked away.

**4** For severe infestations, spray affected plants with insecticidal soap. Repeat applications every ten days for a month. If you've had problems with spider mites before, be prepared to spray as soon as you notice the first symptoms.

# 'JEANNE LAJOIE'
## Miniature Climber

Zones: 5–9; needs protection in colder areas

Size: 4–8 ft. tall

Bloom Time: Early season, with good repeat

Bloom Width: 1 in.

Fragrance: Slight

Thorniness: Moderate

In June, pink flowers appear in profusion on 'Jeanne Lajoie'. The small but double blossoms are laden with forty medium pink petals and a slight fragrance. The high-centered flowers occur singly and in clusters on this vigorous, well-branched rose that can ascend to 8 feet tall. The disease-resistant foliage is small, glossy, and dark green. More winter hardy than other miniatures (and full-sized climbers), 'Jeanne Lajoie' won the American Rose Society Award of Excellence in 1977.

### HOW TO GROW

Plant 'Jeanne Lajoie' in a sunny location in soil that is both well drained and amended with organic matter. For the first three growing seasons, train canes to their supports and prune to remove any dead and diseased wood as it appears. Once the plant is established, remove the oldest canes and cut back remaining stems by two-thirds to three-quarters in late winter or early spring when plants are dormant. Deadhead spent blooms to encourage heavier repeat bloom. 'Jeanne Lajoie' benefits from the application of fungicidal soap in spring. Repeat as needed. Pests such as aphids and mites sometimes are problems. To control, apply an insecticidal soap.

### How to Use

'Jeanne Lajoie' makes an excellent rose for a trellis, which it will swiftly cover. The petite size of its blooms makes this rose a good choice for a trellis in a smaller space, though blooms are so abundant they also show up well from a distance. If allowed to sprawl, it also makes a vigorous hedge or a stand-alone specimen forming a colorful fountain of bloom in the landscape.

## Top Choice

- 'Earthquake, Climbing' is a showy red-and-yellow-striped climber that will complement any garden with a hot color scheme. This vigorous plant, which grows 6 feet tall, has good repeat bloom. Flowers of 'Earthquake, Climbing' take on a pinkish hue in cool weather.

## Planting a Container-Grown Rose

Most miniature roses are sold in containers and need relatively little care at planting because they have an established, if small, root system. Whether miniature or full sized, the planting procedure for container roses is the same. Water the containerized plant before transplanting.

**1** Dig a hole about 1 foot deep and 1 foot wide (or a size equivalent to the pot it came in).

**2** Remove the plant from its pot; loosen the roots, separating them slightly at the ends. If it's rootbound, untangle the roots. With one hand under the plant and roots extending downward, lower it into the hole, adjusting depth as needed so you can set it at the same level it grew in the pot.

**3** Backfill with soil little by little, firming it as you go. Water thoroughly.

**4** Add a layer of mulch around the root zone. Water deeply at least once a week (more right after planting).

# 'SNOW BRIDE'
## Miniature

Zones: 5–9

Size: 15–18 in. tall, 10–14 in. wide

Bloom Time: Mid-season, with good repeat

Bloom Width: 1 in.

Fragrance: Slight

Thorniness: Moderate

'Snow Bride' produces excellent, creamy white minia-ture roses in midseason with good repeat. The small, double flowers are perfect small versions of the classic hybrid tea shape, with high centers, twenty to twenty-two petals, and a slight scent. They're carried on a small, rounded bush. It is disease resistant and winter hardy, with somewhat glossy, medium green leaves. 'Snow Bride' responds well to extra fertilizer and tender loving care. It grows best in mild climates. It won the American Rose Society Award of Excellence in 1983.

### HOW TO GROW
'Snow Bride' prefers at least 6 hours of sun per day. It flowers best in moist, fertile, well-drained soil. Prune in spring as buds begin to swell, cutting canes back by one-half. Deadhead spent flowers (see page 61). Feed in

spring (after pruning) with a complete fertilizer designed for use on roses; repeat after the first blooms have faded to assure a good repeat show.

### HOW TO USE

As with most other miniatures, 'Snow Bride' is perfect as a short hedge. Use the low hedge to line the front walk or edge a patio, or to frame an island bed of taller roses with bright flowers. Where space is limited, grow this rose in a large container; use two to flank a doorway or cluster several on a sunny deck. Its classic, high-centered, hybrid tea form and beautiful white flowers make it a favorite border accent.

## Top Choices

- 'Irresistible', which debuted in 1990, has very full white flowers with a unique, slightly greenish cast.

- 'Pacesetter' bears pure white, fragrant, high-centered blossoms; the buds may be tinted a blush pink. It stands 18 to 24 inches high and received an American Rose Society Award of Excellence in 1981.

## Taylor's Tips

### USING MULCH TO PROMOTE HEALTH

Mulching your miniature roses at the beginning of the growing season is a good practice. It helps maintain the soil's moisture and keeps the temperature cool, especially during a drought. Mulching also helps smother weeds around roses—a good thing, since thorns can make weeding unpleasant.

Coarser mulches such as bark chips last longer, but finer mulches such as shredded leaves provide more organic matter and nutrients, because they break down more quickly. Spread mulches 2 to 4 inches deep.

### TOP-DRESSING

Mulches such as well-rotted manure (aged at least a year) or compost improve the soil and provide high levels of organic matter and nutrients, which give roses a boost. Such nutrient-rich "mulch" materials are called topdressings. Lay down a 1- to 2-inch layer around each plant, spread at least to the drip line of the foliage. Cover with a thin layer of an attractive mulch such as shredded bark or bark chips to minimize weeds.

# 'STARINA'
## Miniature

Zones: 4–9 with adequate winter protection, 6–9 unprotected

Size: 12–16 in. tall, 12 in. wide

Bloom Time: Mid-season, with excellent repeat

Bloom Width: 1 in.

Fragrance: Slight to none

Thorniness: Moderate

Easy to grow and striking to behold, 'Starina' bears vivid orange-red flowers marked by yellow at the base of each petal. The small blooms have thirty-five petals and a slight scent. The flower form is high centered like a hybrid tea rose. Disease resistant and winter hardy (with protection), the bush has a rounded shape and somewhat glossy, dark green leaves. 'Starina' is a dependable repeat bloomer.

### HOW TO GROW

Like most miniature roses, 'Starina' prefers a sunny location sheltered from strong winds. Plant in well-drained soil amended with some organic matter. Prune in spring when buds begin to swell, trimming all canes back by one-half. Deadhead spent flowers to encourage continuous bloom (see page 61). In the unlikely event that disease symptoms appear on the leaves, use fungicidal soap as soon as possible to control. Hose off foliage periodically to discourage insect pests; if stronger measures are required, try insecticidal soap.

### HOW TO USE

As the most popular of all miniature varieties, 'Starina' has been used creatively in a variety of settings. In particular, the dense green leaves and bright orange-red blossoms make it a perfect plant for massing as a luscious, colorful ground cover. Take advantage of its repeat blooms by including it in a border featuring hot-colored flowers; it works well in both formal and informal designs.

## Top Choices

- 'Red Cascade' is a miniature with prolific 1-inch crimson flowers set against a backdrop of bright green foliage. It works well cascading over the sides of a hanging basket, as a ground cover, or as a miniature climber. 'Red Cascade' is 1 foot tall and 3 to 5 feet wide. It received an American Rose Society Award of Excellence in 1976.

- 'Hot Tamale' has larger flowers, to 2½ inches across, with hybrid tea form; they open yellow and change to orange, red, and rose. The plant is also bigger, growing 18 to 22 inches high with a 30-inch spread.

## MINIATURE ROSES IN WINTER

To protect miniature roses from winter weather, applying a loose covering of mulch over the roots works best. Evergreen boughs, leaves, hay, or straw are popular materials. In the South, no such protection is needed.

Plants purchased in the fall can be heeled-in, protected overwinter, and planted in spring. To heel in a rose dig a hole slightly larger than the rootball. Slip the rose from its container and place the plant in the ground at a 45 degree angle. Cover the rootball with soil, then cover the plant with a layer of loose mulch.

## BEDS FULL OF MINIATURES

When mass planting in rock gardens or other locations, space miniature rose plants 12 to 18 inches apart. Fill in spaces between them with mulch, and renew each spring and fall.

# GLOSSARY

**Alba:** A type of old garden rose typically bearing clusters of small, fragrant white flowers.

**Black spot:** A fungal disease that infects many types of roses, causing black spots to form on leaves and ultimately leaves falling from the plant (defoliation). The disease is most severe during wet, warm weather.

**Bonemeal:** Ground raw or steamed bone that is added to the soil as a phosphorous-rich fertilizer.

**Bourbon:** A type of old garden rose with stout, compact habit.

**Bud break:** When a dormant bud begins to elongate and grow.

**Bud eye:** A dormant bud in the axil of a leaf. Bud eyes are used in a form of rose propagation called bud grafting.

**Bud union:** The junction between the understock and the grafted variety above it.

**Cane:** A long, often unbranched, woody stem.

**Centifolia:** A type of old garden rose, also called the cabbage rose, similar in appearance to the gallica rose.

**Chlorosis:** The reduction of chlorophyll in a leaf, resulting in a yellowish appearance. Chlorosis can have many causes, including nutrient deficiencies and disease.

**Crown:** The region of the bud union near the soil line where the understock and the grafted variety are joined.

**Crown borer:** An insect that tunnels into shoots and stems to lay eggs. The emerging larvae then feed on the surrounding healthy plant tissue.

**Cultivar:** A variety of plant that has persisted through cultivation and been given a name. An example of a cultivar is the rose 'New Dawn'.

**Damask:** A type of old garden rose cultivated at least since the time of the Crusades. Most bloom once, though some repeat in late summer.

**Deadheading:** Removing faded blossoms from the stem before seeds begin to set.

**Double blossom:** A blossom that has many more than the usual number of petals.

**Floribunda:** A class of modern rose derived from crossing hybrid polyantha and hybrid tea roses. The flowers resemble hybrid teas in form and color, but are smaller and borne in clusters.

**Fungicide:** A substance that inhibits the growth of or kills specific fungi.

**Foundation planting:** Planting along the foundation or base of a building to conceal or camouflage it.

**Gallica:** An ancient type of old garden rose, usually with rich fragrance and colors ranging from pink to red.

**Grafting:** A method of propagating plants in which two different plants are fused together.

**Hip:** The vitamin C–rich fruit of a rose.

**Humus:** Well-decomposed organic matter.

**Insecticidal soap**: A combination of sodium or potassium salts and oils usually derived from vegetable sources. They are used to control soft-bodied insects and mites, but are largely ineffective against other insects such as beetles, wasps, and flies.

**Japanese beetle:** A beetle about ½ inch long with copper-brown wing covers and a metallic green head and prothorax (upper portion of body).

**Lateral:** A stem or flower that rises from the side of a larger stem.

**Loppers:** A pruning tool with long handles and a cutting blade used to trim stems and branches that are 1 to 2 inches in diameter.

**Mildew:** A fungal disease. The mildew that attacks roses is most often a type of powdery mildew that begins with a curling of the leaves. As the infection advances, a white powdery coating appears on the leaves, on the buds, and near thorns on the canes.

**Miniature:** A group of roses usually less than 18 inches tall with smaller-than-normal leaves and flowers.

**Node:** The area of a stem where leaves arise.

**pH:** A measure of the acidity or alkalinity of a solution as plotted on a scale of 0 to 14 with 7 being neutral. Measurements less than 7 are acidic while those greater than 7 are alkaline.

**Polyantha:** A group of hardy, old-garden-rose hybrids with a dwarf habit and small flowers.

**Own-root rose:** A rose that has not been grafted and therefore is growing on its own roots rather than those of another.

**Quartered:** A rose blossom with three, four, or five radial segments.

**Recurrent bloom:** Blooming periodically throughout the growing season.

**Repeat-blooming rose:** Any rose that has a nonblooming period between its spring and fall flowering periods.

**Rugosa:** A group of hardy, disease-resistant hybrids derived from the beach rose (*Rosa rugosa*) with textured glossy leaves and bristly thorns along the canes.

**Rust, rose:** A fungal disease that manifests as bright orange dots on the undersides of leaves with yellow dots on the tops of leaves. The disease is most prevalent during moist, warm, but not hot weather. It sometimes occurs in the Northeast but is most severe in the Pacific Northwest and during winter in southern California.

**Semidouble:** A blossom with more than the normal number of petals but less than twice as many. In roses, a blossom with from twelve to twenty-four petals.

**Sport:** A genetic mutation in a developing bud that gives rise to a branch that is notably different from the rest of the plant. Many varieties began as sports that were then propagated.

**Stamen:** The male portion of a flower consisting of a threadlike structure called the filament and the pollen-bearing sac called the anther.

**Stratifying:** Placing seeds in a moist, cold environment for a predetermined period to satisfying the dormancy requirement in order to grow.

**Suckers:** In grafted roses, canes rising from beneath bud union; in species or own-root roses, canes rising from underground portions of roots or stems.

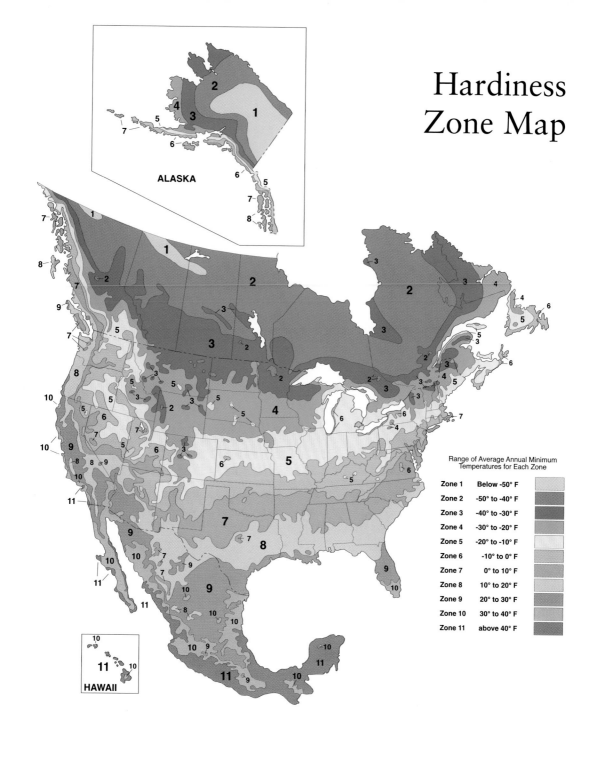

# Hardiness Zone Map

**ALASKA**

**HAWAII**

Range of Average Annual Minimum
Temperatures for Each Zone

| Zone | Temperature |
|------|-------------|
| Zone 1 | Below -50° F |
| Zone 2 | -50° to -40° F |
| Zone 3 | -40° to -30° F |
| Zone 4 | -30° to -20° F |
| Zone 5 | -20° to -10° F |
| Zone 6 | -10° to 0° F |
| Zone 7 | 0° to 10° F |
| Zone 8 | 10° to 20° F |
| Zone 9 | 20° to 30° F |
| Zone 10 | 30° to 40° F |
| Zone 11 | above 40° F |

# INDEX

# Photography & Illustration Credits

H. Abernathy/H. Armstrong Roberts
Front Cover

ALD photo Inc.
12, 14, 18, 28, 56, 76, 90, 92, 96, 100, 102, 106

David Cavagnaro
10, 54

Crandall & Crandall
112

Thomas E. Eltzroth
22

Derek Fell
Back cover, title page, 24, 32, 44, 50, 60, 62, 64, 68, 80, 72, 74, 80, 82, 84, 104, 108

Holt Studios International/ Gordon Roberts
94

Holt Studios International/ Ivor Speed
78

Bill Johnson
20, 38, 48, 110

Judy McKeon
52

Jerry Pavia
16, 30, 36, 40, 42, 58, 66, 86, 88, 114, 118

Richard Shiell
26, 34, 98, 116

Illustrator: Beverly Duncan

## Storey Communications, Inc.
## Pownal, Vermont

*President:* M. John Storey
*Executive Vice President:* Martha M. Storey
*Chief Operating Officer:* Dan Reynolds
*Director of Custom Publishing:* Deirdre Lynch
*Project Manager:* Barbara Weiland
*Author:* Penelope O'Sullivan
*Book Design:* Betty Kodela
*Design Assistance:* Erin Lincourt, Jen Rork
*Horticulture Editor:* Charles W. G. Smith